IMPROVE Y
ENGLISH ...

Constance Hawkins
Senior lecturer in English at Bedford College of Higher Education

Roger Strangwick
Head of English at Bedford College of Higher Education

Longman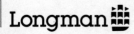

Longman Group UK Limited,
*Longman House, Burnt Mill, Harlow,
Essex CM20 2JE, England
and Associated Companies throughout the world.*

© Longman Group UK Limited 1990

First published 1990

*Set in 11/13 point Ehrhardt Roman, Linotron 202
Produced by Longman Group (FE) Ltd.
Printed in Hong Kong.*

ISBN 0 582 35571 0

Acknowledgement

The Vehicle Application Form on page 92
is Crown copyright and is reproduced with the
permission of the Controller of Her Majesty's Stationery
Office.

CONTENTS

UNIT THREE   SORT OUT YOUR IDEAS   61

UNIT FOUR   FILL IN FORMS   87

UNIT SIX THE WAY YOU TALK 135

UNIT ONE

TAKE A MESSAGE

TAKE A MESSAGE

1 How to make sense of what you hear

ANNOUNCEMENTS

No public announcement is easy to take in the first time you hear it:

- You don't realise an announcement is being made until it is half over.
- When you try to listen, there always seems to be someone next to you talking loudly enough to be heard a mile away in a thunderstorm. (The same person usually talks to you, non-stop, when you are trying to talk to someone else on the telephone.)
- The microphone and speakers will be crackling and whining like a car radio under a railway bridge.

There are two things in your favour:

- A good announcer reads any message quite slowly.
- Only a bad announcer reads a message just once.

When you realise an announcement is being made, OR if someone is dictating a message which you are trying to write down:

- Never worry about words you have missed.
- Concentrate instead on the words you hear now.
- Then wait (or ask) for the words you missed to be repeated.
- Or ask the nearest official person for advice. Officials are likely to know what is going on and where the fire escape is, or which train is pulling into the station.
- Whether the announcement is about a bomb threat or a bargain offer of dustbin liners, listen carefully: it could suddenly become of interest or even importance to you.

1 Try to sort out:
   what is going on
   where
   why
   what to do about it

2 **Count how many important points there are in the announcement.**
   Then you can check later that you have remembered them all. The main facts in this message are in <u>underlined type</u> and are numbered:

> (1)   (2)
> This is a <u>police announcement.</u> <u>A lorry carrying chemicals has</u>
> (3)
> <u>overturned</u> in <u>George Street</u> and has spilled its load.
> (4)
> The area affected has been <u>closed to traffic</u> and will remain
> (5)
> closed <u>for at least three hours.</u>
> (6)
> Through-traffic should follow the <u>Police Diversion signs.</u>
> No traffic will be allowed in the area until further notice.

1 Count the main points

Decide how many important points (or claims) are being made in this advertisement.

> New-Skin Face Creams give new life to tired skin. A new formula — based on rose petals, passion fruit, goats' milk and an Exotic Secret Ingredient — feeds in moisture to protect delicate skin from sun and wind and give it a soft, healthy glow. Choose from six delicate fragrances! New-Skin Face Creams: the face creams for Real Men!

2 Practise making an announcement

Record the following announcements on tape.

Try to get a different person to record each message, so that you have to get used to different voices when you play the tape back. Each message should be read clearly, a little more slowly than normal reading speed, and TWICE, before the next one begins. Leave a short pause between each announcement.

a) The train now arriving at platform eight is the 11.20 inter-city express calling at St Albans, Bedford, Leicester, Nottingham and Derby. Passengers for St Albans and Bedford should use the two rear coaches only.

   The refreshment car is located between the third and fourth carriages.

b) Shortcircuit Superstores have bargains for all the family! Junior Dungeon Packs are now selling in our Toddlers' Corner for only three pounds — that's one pound fifty less than the manufacturer's recommended retail price. Plastic leg-irons, rack and thumbscrews are all included to keep youngsters amused for hours!

   Older Do-It-Yourselfers will find our ready-to-assemble Lunar Laser and Microwave Kits on sale on the second floor — all at crazy prices!

c) Will the owner of the dark blue van with the blue roof light, registration number G653 ERP, please remove it from the rear entrance to the bank as it is causing an obstruction. Thank you.

d) Vote today for Nerinder Dawson, your candidate from the People's Party. A vote for Nerinder is a vote for lower taxes and equal rights.

   Polling booths are open until ten o'clock tonight. Remember! Vote for Nerinder Dawson and the People's Party *now*!

3 Take in the information

If you are working with a group of people, get the others to write out, and then record, one announcement each. Use the same cassette tape as before and still repeat each message twice.

Until the tape is played, only the writer and your lecturer should know what each announcement says.

If you are working on your own, record a series of television commercials instead. About ten would give you enough material to work on later.

Make a note of how many announcements were recorded, then play back the tape at random, so that no one knows which message you will hear.

Play the tape long enough to hear a complete announcement, counting the number of important points in it as you listen. Then stop the tape. Now write down as much of the information as you can remember.

Compare what you have written with what others in your group have remembered.

Replay the recording to check how well you remembered the announcement.

4 Take in the information

Continue listening to the taped messages, stopping the tape at random, counting the important points, and then writing down all you can remember.

If you can memorise the announcement easily, increase the number you listen to at one time to three, or even four.

Repeat the exercise until you have worked on all the announcements.

5 Take in the information

Record the announcements made on the radio just before the five o'clock news. Then record the news reading.

a) Play the announcements TWICE and count all the facts you hear. Then stop the tape and write down all the facts you can remember.

b) Now listen to the taped news reading. Again, listen to it TWICE and count the facts as you listen. Then stop the tape and write down all you can remember of each news item.

c) If you are working in a group, compare what each of you remembered of the announcements and the news.

d) Then check what you have written by listening to the tape again.

Repeat this task, recording:

- more news bulletins
- television commercials
- short extracts from radio and television programmes
- extracts from instruction manuals

This is a good memory-training exercise, but how much you remember depends on many things:

> how complicated the message is
> whether other things stop you from concentrating
> how tired you feel
> how interested you are in the information
> how well you understand what you hear

Never be worried if you are not remembering as much as you hoped. Have a short rest before you try again — and <u>count the main points you need to remember</u> in each announcement.

FOLLOWING INSTRUCTIONS

If someone at home or at work asks you to go to the post office for two first-class stamps, one second-class stamp, three black biros with fine points, five blue biros with medium points and a copy of the *Radio Times*, do you always:

A) get all the things exactly right?
B) remember, *before* you go, that it is early closing day so the post office will be shut?
C) get the right stamps, the wrong biros and forget the magazine?
D) get half-way there, bump into a friend, have a quick chat, then forget where you were going and wonder what it was you had to get?

If you answer A or B, you are very efficient.
If you answer C or D, it simply means that, like the rest of us, you have a perfectly normal human tendency to:

> mis-hear what people say;
> misunderstand what you are told;
> dislike asking people to explain or repeat what they say.

1 When you **do not** hear or understand instructions properly:

- ask for them to be repeated
- ask the meaning of words you do not understand
- ask for a **map**, a **diagram**, or a **list** to help you to understand (and therefore remember) what you have to do.

Asking for help like this might take time — but it will also show how thorough and sensible you are. It might be embarrassing too — but far less embarrassing than having to come back half an hour later, unable to find whoever or whatever you were sent to fetch.

2 When you **do** hear and understand your instructions:

- first **count** the number of things you have to do
- then make a **list** of them, if you have not been given one

Write down:

> **what** you are to deliver / collect / do;
> **where** you are to go;
> **who** you must deal with;
> **when** exactly you have to do the task / get back;
> **special instructions**, if any.

Make your list short, like the one below, and number the points.

what ⟶	1 Collect Mr Cohen's parcel
	2 + £5 from the Finance Office
where ⟶	3 Go to the <u>main</u> post office
special instructions	4 Register the parcel
who ⟶	5 Give receipt + change to Mrs Chaney
when ⟶	6 Be back by 2

3 Before you start, think about what you have to do, step by step. You may not have been given enough details and if you ask sensible questions *now* it shows you are alert.

Do you know the

> brand,
> reference number,
> size,
> colour,
> flavour,
> price?

If you are unable to get *exactly* what is wanted, are you to get the closest alternative you can find?

If you have to deliver a letter to Jean Price and she is out, should you:

- leave the letter for her and come straight back?
- wait for her and, if so, for how long?
- return, bringing the letter with you?

If you *do* see her, should you wait for an answer?

6 Check the instructions

What information is missing from these instructions?

a) Please leave 3 pints a day each day except Sunday.
b) Turn left at the post office, right after you have passed Wool-
   worths, then take the third turning and you'll find Littlewoods
   at the far end by the traffic lights.
c) Take these along to the Post Room and tell Miss Sangherra
   I want all of them to go first-class mail. Of course it may all
   be locked up as she finishes at 4.30.
d) Can you get me a battery from Stores? Be quick, it closes soon
   — and take a trolley, those things are heavy!

7 Follow these instructions

Carry out the instructions given below.

Go to the nearest railway station and find out the time of the first train to:

Manchester
or Glasgow
or Birmingham
or Truro

which leaves next Wednesday morning between 8.30 and 11.00 a.m.

Find out if you would have to change trains. If so, find out where you would change, and at what time.

Find out the cost of the cheapest return ticket.

Then find out the cost of a return ticket which would allow you to stay for seven days before coming back.

If there is more than one way of getting there by train, choose the cheapest way, but make a note of how much any other would cost.

Make a list of these facts, then report all this to someone else AND describe, briefly, any problems you had in getting the information.

8 Follow these instructions

Make a list of FOUR items your partner wants you to look for at a nearby department store, supermarket or Do-It-Yourself store.

Before you go, make sure you know all the sizes, brands, colours and other details. Each of your items should be from a different section of the store.

Then go to the store and make a list of the prices of these four items. Write down details, too, of any similar items in stock which you think are more attractive *or* better value for money.

If any of the four items are not in stock, get prices, and other details, of the best alternatives you can find.

Report back on the facts you have discovered *and* on any problems you have had in finding the goods.

9 Find out the information

Now ask your partner to find out these facts about your local college, OR the place where you work:

> the telephone number(s)
> the fire regulations
> the car park size
> the canteen's opening hours

Discuss the best ways of finding this information before your partner starts. Your partner should report back with facts *and* any problems there were in finding them.

2 How to pass a message on

At a children's party, it can be fun to pass a message down the line in whispers and see just how *wrong* the final version is.

In real life, getting a message wrong is no joke.

Your pride and perhaps your job will depend on getting the message right.

Listen carefully.
You still have to concentrate on:

> **what**
> **where**
> **who**
> **when**

just as you did when following instructions. But now there are not just *things* to deal with. Now you have to sort out somebody's words and ideas, pass them on, and perhaps bring back a reply.

To remember everything you must:

> understand all the **words** used (including technical words, if possible);
> understand all the **ideas**;
> *write down* any **facts** you are given.

If there is anything you do not understand, **ask** what it means.

If you have to tell Mr Jackson that Mrs de Soto wants a ratio of two measures of freeze dried caffeine to one of sucrose in 0.25 of a litre of H_2O at 11.10, you might find the message a bit hard to remember.

But when you understand that Mrs de Soto simply wants two spoons of instant coffee and one spoon of sugar in roughly half a pint of water, during her mid-morning break — you should find the message easier to deal with!

You will also realise that Mrs de Soto likes to use rather 'technical' language, and be ready to concentrate harder next time she asks you to deliver a message.

Even if the message is simply how to make the coffee — or that Mr Jackson should deal with the three blue files but send the two green ones to Head Office, write the message down. Otherwise, between your starting point and Mr Jackson's office, you could muddle the number of blue and green folders beyond all hope of rescue.

The perfect messenger:

- admits (even to himself) that he does not know everything;
- listens carefully;
- says 'Goodmorning Mrs Jackson' *before* delivering the message;
- asks for an explanation when things are not clear;
- asks *two* or *three* people on the staff how jobs are usually done (one person might give you bad advice!);
- does what he is *told*, without delay.

10 Messages you can work on

If possible, work in a group of three people for the following activities, each of you taking one of the parts.

Make up any extra information you need.

a) A parent takes a sick child to the doctor's surgery and tells the receptionist exactly what seems to be wrong, when the symptoms started and what has been done about them so far.

   The receptionist makes notes on all this, including these people's <u>invented</u> names and goes to another room to tell the doctor what was said.

   The doctor then checks this information with the parent.

b) A customer takes a suit back to the dry-cleaners to complain that they have damaged it. The assistant writes down the <u>invented</u> name, address, complaint, the date when the suit was brought in, and when it was collected.

   The assistant goes away to tell the supervisor exactly what has happened.

   The supervisor then checks this information with the customer.

c) A pedestrian has witnessed a road accident and describes, to a police constable, what happened.

   The constable reports to an inspector everything the pedestrian has said.

   The inspector then checks this information with the pedestrian.

11 Pass on the message

Work in groups of three for this.

Choose a partner to be your messenger and send the other person to another room to wait for the message. Then:

• choose one of the three situations from pages 19–20
• invent all the details needed, and make a note of them
• tell your partner the message which has to be delivered
• do *not* let your partner see your notes

Your partner must:

• ask you to explain anything about the message which is not clear
• ask you for any extra information which may be needed
• write down any facts which have to be remembered
• deliver the message to the other person waiting to receive it.

The person working as Message Receiver should:

• ask for an explanation if anything is confusing
• ask for any information which has been missed out
• make notes about what the message said.

The three of you should then compare:

• the message you tried to send;
• the message the Deliverer thought was being sent;
• the message the Receiver believed had been sent.

If all of these are exactly the same, you have worked very efficiently.

Now choose a different message from the list, taking it in turns to be Sender, Deliverer and Receiver of the message.

Three situations you can work on

1 You are Pat's mother. Leave this urgent telephone message with your partner, who then has to deliver it to Pat.

Pat's father has been taken ill at work and is now in hospital, in intensive care. You are going to the hospital straight away, but Pat does not have a door key, so you will leave one with your neighbour.

Pat must collect your two younger children on the way home, tell them what has happened, collect the key from the neighbour, prepare the tea, look after a pet and wait for another telephone call from you.

Invent: the names of people, the hospital, the ward
  the times and places Pat is to collect the two younger
    children
  what is wrong with their father
  what Pat has to do for the pet
  what is to be prepared for tea

2 You are the director in charge of repairs and maintenance at a garage which has two local branches.

In your office at the main branch you have just checked the staff time-sheet for last week. You noticed that one mechanic at the other branch was away one day last week and was late for work every other day.

Also, a furious customer has just telephoned to complain that a van sent in for a 20,000-mile service last week has just broken down 50 miles away, fully loaded.

Work sheets show that the same mechanic did the work on the van. You are very angry and if there is no good explanation for these problems the mechanic will be sacked.

Tell all of this to your workshop supervisor, who must then take your message to the Message Receiver, who is the mechanic involved.

Invent: the names of people, firms and branches
  which day the mechanic was away
  a description of the van (so the mechanic will know
    whether he did do the work on it)
  the time the mechanic should have started work
  the time when the mechanic actually arrived each day

3 The mechanic who was in trouble in the last situation explains everything to the workshop supervisor, who reports back to the director.

Invent: this explanation.

■ ADVICE

It is almost always the Deliverer who has the hardest job to do. As well as remembering what to say, that person must change the tone of voice *and* the words used to suit the message being delivered.

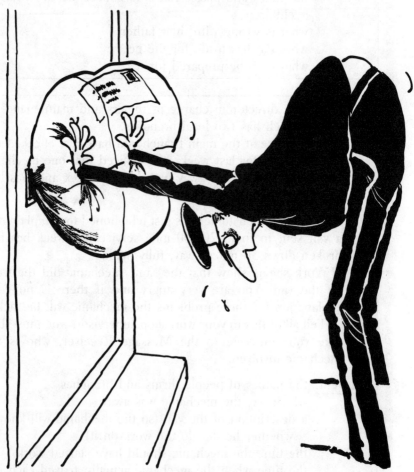

It is almost always the Deliverer who has the hardest job to do

TAKING A TELEPHONE MESSAGE

Often the message you have to deal with will come by telephone. If you have to answer the telephone at work, at your local sports club, or anywhere 'official':

first say the name of the firm, club or organisation;
then say 'Good morning/afternoon/evening';
then, once again, write down
what
where
who
when
the message is about.

Most firms have a special form for taking down telephone messages, to help you remember to write down the most vital things.

TELEPHONE MESSAGE

TO: _____   DEPARTMENT: _____

FROM: Name _____

Address _____

_____

_____

Tel. No. _____

MESSAGE: _____

_____

_____

_____

_____

MESSAGE TAKEN BY: _____

DATE: _____   TIME: _____

---

12 Take a telephone message

Copy out the telephone message form, then use it to write down the message left by Pat's mother (on page 19).

Invent the names, date, time and any other facts needed.

Help yourself to remember

The manager gave you an urgent message to deliver, then rushed off to meet a customer. Before you could write the message down you had to answer the telephone twice.

You have now forgotten every word of the message *and* who it was for.

■ ADVICE

Relax.

Breathe — and think — slowly and carefully. If you panic your brain will close down!

Imagine exactly what happened when the manager gave you the message.

Think of the room you were in, the expression on his face, the papers he was holding.

Try to 'see' it again in your thoughts; try to 'hear' the tone of voice he used.

Think of what you were both saying *before* he gave you the message.

Was the message nice or nasty?

Did you need to leave the building to deliver it?

When he left, where were you standing, which way were you facing, what were you holding?

Repeat your movements.

Go back to the room where you were given the message. Do again exactly what you think you did before.

If everything fails, admit it without any more delay.

Try to contact your manager quickly.

Apologise.

Explain *briefly* what made you forget.

Write down the message when he repeats it!

And, *next* time, let the telephone ring for a minute longer so that you can make a note of at least some of the message you have to remember.

You see a van knock a cyclist off her bike on a country road. The van doesn't stop. Its registration number is D763 FFH but you have nothing to write it down on, or with, and will probably forget it as you rush to help the injured cyclist.

In an old-fashioned film there would be lipstick, or a pot of paint, or even blood which you could use to write the number — but now there is no lipstick, paint or blood to spare.

■ ADVICE

1 **Make the letters in the registration number stand for words:**
D. . . FFH could stand for
Dragons Frighten Foolish Hamsters
or
Dial For Fast Help
A saying — especially a silly one — is easier to remember than a row of letters.

2 **Use the names and ages of people you know to help you remember** letters *and* numbers:

Daljit's father is 76
+ 3 neighbours, Frances, Fred and Harbinder
= D763 FFH

3 **Try to make up one or two words which use all the letters you have to remember**, and in the right order:
D F F H could become
DeaF FisH

13 How to remember names and numbers

Invent ways of your own to help you remember as many of these six items as you can:

C 252 PRO
E 654 SKG
Bletchley 25252
John Albert Fitzroy Conrad
200 grams of flour, 100 grams sugar, 2 eggs, 100 grams
   butter
Oldham 35242

Suppose that, however hard you try, you keep forgetting instructions, and keep getting things wrong. You feel clumsy, useless, and sometimes stay away from college (or work) because you can't cope.

■ ADVICE

1 Never sulk, or lose your temper.

2 Realise that every person there probably felt just as useless for the first month or two.

3 Ask a friendly person on the staff to talk to you about your worries.
  You may learn:
     that you are doing better than you think
     that you have been given work which is too hard for a beginner
     easier ways of doing some of the things you are worried about

4 *Never* try to keep a lot of information in your head.
  Efficient people make a note of things they must remember.

5 Learn *one* section of each job, thoroughly, at a time.

6 Ask *why* each step of the job has to be done, if you do not know already.

7 Practise, asking someone with more experience to watch you and give you advice *only* if you get stuck.

8 Always try to finish one job before you start another.

9 Listen carefully to instructions. Concentrating sensibly on what people say is a valuable skill.

3 How to get it down on paper

14 Write an announcement

Read again the announcements on pages 9 and 10. Then, working on your own, write an announcement which could be made from a police van's loudspeaker, based on the following information.

> A man has escaped from the local prison. He was serving ten years for armed robbery and shooting a bank clerk. He is dangerous and if he is identified he should not be tackled.

Invent: a description of the man
  what action should be taken if he is seen

Record your announcement, then listen carefully to the recording. Could your message *and* the way *you* read it be made clearer?

15 Write an announcement

Write an announcement which could be made during a football match, or open air concert, based on the following information.

> People are asked to move out of the Riverside Stand.
> They can use three of the exits, but not the fourth one.
> They should leave the stand calmly, there is no need to panic.
> There will be officials waiting outside who will lead them to another stand where they can watch the rest of the match or competition.

Invent: a reason for asking them to move
  numbers or letters for the four exits

Record your announcement, then listen to the recording. Would other people understand exactly:

> what was happening?
> what you were asking them to do?

16 Find the facts

a) Read about this rather bad week in the life of an office worker.

> It's been such a week! First the pipes burst. Well, that didn't actually happen till Thursday, but it was just about the most awful thing that happened.

It snowed from Sunday night till Wednesday morning, almost non-stop. The bus was an hour late on Tuesday, so I didn't get to work till gone ten o'clock. Then there were only two of us to do everything; Joe and Dean rang to say they couldn't get in: the roads were blocked from Stotfold and Willington; not even a snow plough could get through.

Of course it was even worse on Wednesday. My bus came along all right — forty minutes late of course, but it did turn up. Not like Monday, when it didn't arrive at all: I waited nearly an hour at that bus stop, from 8.15 until 9.10, then I gave up and went home. It took another hour before I got the feeling back in my feet.

Anyway, on Wednesday I got to work all right, but I was the only one who did — apart from Mrs Dennis, and she lives in the flat over the office. She sent me home at three and just as well she did: I caught the last bus to get through to Clapham! I haven't been back to work since, and today's Friday.

The one good thing about the whole week was that the man came to repair the fridge on Monday afternoon and, because of the trouble with the buses, I was there when he called. He didn't bother to let me know he was coming on Monday, of course, but at least if we get a heat wave the icecream won't melt!

b) List the **facts** given in what you have just read, **in the order** they actually happened.

Write the name of each day as a heading, then list underneath it the main events of that day.

Include names and times, but leave out personal details (such as where Mrs Dennis lived).

17 Take a telephone message

Copy out the Telephone Message form used on page 21, then use it to write down the message Dean sent in, in exercise 16. Invent names, date, time and any other facts needed.

18 See things from a different point of view

Write a *short* description of the awful week described in exercise 16, **as if you were the driver of the bus the office worker was waiting for each day**. Write it in the form of a work report, with a separate entry for each day of the week.

4 Words: health

Medicine and Me

People never believe me when I say I feel off-colour: they just grin at me as though I'm a well-known hypochondriac and say 'Oh yes!' in a very irritating way.

Mum hasn't believed I've been ill since I told her I had tonsillitis, when I was six. I tried to whisper hoarsely but the vacuum cleaner was switched on so I had to shout to make her hear me.

The trouble is, I never get things badly enough to get any sympathy. People all around me go down with influenza, bronchitis, even pneumonia, but I just have a sore throat and a sniffle and have to struggle on. Everyone else gets the grapes and the flowers, I just pay for the Get Well cards.

I have taken a friend to hospital a few times, so I've spent a few interesting hours waiting in Casualty or in the Outpatients Department. You see all sorts of interesting cases being wheeled in on stretchers. It's quite dramatic: a broken leg on its way to the Orthopaedic Department; a rather nasty black eye waiting for an icepack; a toddler allergic to cats, who wouldn't stop cuddling all the neighbourhood moggies — and had an attack of asthma.

When I have to go to the the doctor's surgery it's always for something dull and routine, like renewing my prescription for anti-histamine tablets every spring because of my hayfever. I can tell the receptionist thinks I'm wasting the doctor's time by the way she looks at me when I tell her what's wrong.

The most dramatic thing I ever needed was an anti-tetanus injection after I trod on the garden rake.

I daydream about being a famous athlete and having the best osteopath in the country to treat my backache when I've played too much polo. Or about seeing my dietician every month at her Harley Street clinic, when I have chronic anaemia because of overwork and too many canteen sandwiches.

Really I know that I shall never be the centre of attention, nursed with tender loving care at an expensive convalescent home in Torquay. Maybe I ought to be a blood donor. At least then I'd get some tea and biscuits.

19 Check the meanings

Working on your own OR with a partner, check the meanings and the spelling of all the underlined words in the 'Medicine and Me' passage.

Then discuss (*or* write down) what you think of the person who is talking in the passage, and what you think about his or her ideas on being ill.

20 Make sense of what you hear

a) Talk to someone who has been to hospital because of an illness or an accident.
   Find out from them all you can about:

> the symptoms
> the hospital
> the staff
> the size of the ward
> the treatment received
> how the person felt about going to hospital

b) Then go to the Reference section of the nearest library and find out all you can about the illness or injury this person had.
   Ask the librarian to help you find the books you need, and write down the most important facts you find.

c) Then tell the rest of your group about:

> the person you interviewed
> the illness or injury
> what you were told about the hospital
> what you found out from the library

21 Put it in writing

Write the diary of one day in the life of a hospital doctor or nurse. Write at least half a page and include some of the underlined words from the 'Medicine and Me' passage.

5 Check your punctuation: capital letters and full stops

CAPITAL LETTERS

People are sometimes uncertain about when to use a capital letter instead of a small one.

■ ADVICE

Make sure you have a good reason for using a capital letter.

Do not use one just because a word seems important in a sentence.

Use a capital letter for these reasons:

■ **For the word 'I'** — every time you write it, *even* in the middle of a sentence

> We worked hard on that building site last January. After it was finished Jim got promoted, Fred got a bonus, and I got flu.

■ **For initials** — of people *and* (usually) things

> When Dr J. C. Mitchell's car broke down on the M1 she had to ring the AA for help.

■ **To begin the name of a day or month**

> On Saturday, 18th April Fitzroy Clarke got himself a new job, a celebration drink and a hangover.

■ **To begin the first word in any sentence** — whatever that word is

> Under the bonnet is the engine of my dreams.
> or
> The engine of my dreams is under that bonnet.

■ **To begin EVERY word in the name of a person or place**

person	King George and George King.
	both lived near
place	Buckingham Palace Road,
	and both of them liked feeding the ducks in
	London's Hyde Park

Important: it is wrong to write 'Hyde park' or 'George king'. The second (and the third) word in a name needs a capital letter too.

■ **To begin all the main words** (and the **first** one) **in any title**
of a:

> **magazine** or **newspaper** — Darts and Dominoes Weekly
> **book** — The Secret Diary of Adrian Mole

of a:

> **group** — Dire Straits
> **sports team** — Manchester United
> **film** — The Killing of Sister George
> **club** — West Bickerstaff Pekinese and Poodle Association

of a:

> **lord** or **lady** — the Earl and Countess of Finchley
> **king** or **queen** — Queen Elizabeth II of Great Britain

of a:

> **brand name** — Ford Fiesta
> **firm** or **organisation** — Duston District Council

■ **To begin the first word someone says out loud**

> She said, crossly, 'No, I can't lend you five pounds.'

22 Put in the capital letters

Check carefully where the capital letters happen in the next four lines.

> Ramsthorpe General Hospital is in the middle of Russell Hall Park and, more important to some of the staff, just a few yards from The Goat and Garter, which sells good Lancashire hotpot and Ramsthorpe Brewery's finest pale ale.

Now check where — and why — 33 extra capital letters are needed in the rest of the story:

I went to see Zac in hospital on tuesday. He'd been driving too fast down the a57 to salford in the fog and he hit a grey austin metro which was driving without lights.

I knew he was in the John hinchcliffe ward, in one of the new blocks in Russell hall park. it was odd that everyone i saw there looked over seventy but i marched in with my bunch of grapes and a copy of motorcycle news. Then the matron came and told me i was in Ramsthorpe district council's new charterhouse home for the elderly. she said the john Hinchcliffe ward was in russel block, right next to the driveway to the Goat and garter.

When i found it; visiting time was nearly up and zac said, 'next time, spend a bit less time in the pub on the way in! i could tell he was feeling better. patients they call them. zac's never been patient in his life!

FULL STOPS

You have to use full stops so that people can make sense of what you have written.

> ■ ADVICE
>
> Divide what you write into groups of words, so that every group makes sense and has a complete idea inside it.
>
> Put a full stop at the end of each group of words, to show it is finished.
>
> Then anyone reading it gets your message without getting confused.

23 Put in full stops and capital letters

In this piece of writing, each group of words is separated from the next one by a diagonal line.

Write it out yourself, putting:
a full stop instead of each diagonal line,
AND a capital letter at the beginning of each new group of words.

> On Thursday when I went to see him Zac was much better / he was sitting up in bed and waved to me as I went in / he still couldn't talk a lot but he didn't need any more painkilling injections / a nurse had told him he had to have a blood transfusion when he was first admitted / it seems he'd been given three pints of blood, but he couldn't remember a thing about it.

Then read what you have written, working out carefully *why* each diagonal line was put in that particular place.

A group of words which makes sense on its own like this is a sentence.

You have to organise very carefully everything you write — otherwise people just won't be able to understand you. So split up your words into sentences, giving each one

- a capital letter at the beginning AND
- a full stop at the end,

like using an On/Off switch.

Wrong

> By Zac's bed were ten Get Well cards, a huge teddy bear and two girls from the youth club wearing a blue ribbon and a label saying 'We miss you Zac' the teddy bear was a present from all the girls on his YTS course.

In that last paragraph there has to be a full stop after the word 'club' and 'wearing' should begin with a capital letter. Why is it confusing without them?

24 Put in full stops and capital letters

Ask a friend to read out a short newspaper article to you, slowly, so that you can write it down as it is read out. Think carefully about where the full stops and capital letters should go. Then compare your work with the newspaper article to check whether you used them in the same places.

If you are working on your own, record the article on tape, reading it slowly. A day or so later, play the tape and write down what you hear. Do this later to give yourself time to forget just where the sentences ended.

6 Get it right: 'was' and 'were'

Use **was** with these words:

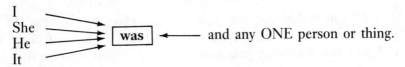

I
She
He
It
was ◀——— and any ONE person or thing.

But use **were** with these:

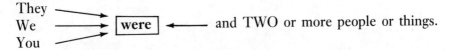

They
We
You
were ◀——— and TWO or more people or things.

I **was** hitchhiking to the concert with Jim.
(because **was** is only really about the word 'I')

---

but

Tom and Jerry **were** hitchhiking there.
(because **were** is about TWO people at the same time)

Who **was** that lady I saw you with last night?
(because you are asking about ONE person)

---

but

Who **were** those idiots who stole a milk float as a get-away car?
(because TWO OR MORE idiots stole it)

---

25 Put in WAS or WERE

Decide whether 'was' or 'were' should go in each of the spaces in these sentences:

When you _____ ill I _____ so worried. No, of course I didn't think you _____ going to die. I just didn't know who _____ going to do the housework. I can't do it, with my bad back.

Just visiting you in hospital _____ bad enough. I _____ always upset by the smell of hospital wards and the disinfectant in that one _____ so strong, no germ _____ going to survive there for long and it _____n't fun for us visitors, I can tell you.

Then you _____ not much of a talker when I _____ there. You _____ just lying there, dozing, when I _____ missing Coronation Street and _____ dying for a cup of tea. And I _____ going to have to wait twenty minutes for a bus when we _____ all sent out in the rain.

All you said to me one night _____ 'Have you watered the pot plants?' You _____n't worried about how I _____ feeling. You and that woman in the next bed _____ only interested in how soon you _____ going to get rid of us visitors and get your cocoa!

TAKE IN WHAT YOU READ

TAKE IN WHAT YOU READ

1 How to work out what it means

ADVERTISEMENTS

An advertisement has to tell you:

> **what** is for sale (+ make/size/colour)
> **where** to buy it
> **when** to buy it
> **how** to buy it
> **how much** it costs

These facts are needed even in **classified advertisements**, sometimes called 'small ads', like this one:

> **Portable Toshiba** b/w TV, 12 in., nearly new £40 o.n.o.
> Tel. Bradford 80372

AND they are needed

> in full-page advertisements
> in handbills (or leaflets)
> in television commercials
> in posters like the one opposite

You have to be told enough about whatever is for sale to decide if it is what you want; so the television set is described above as

> black and white
> with a 12 inch screen

and the poster tells you that Purple Sound is a reggae group, not jazz, folk or brass band.

When ———————→

Where————————→

What
is for sale ———→

**How
much**
it costs ⟍

How
to get it ⟋

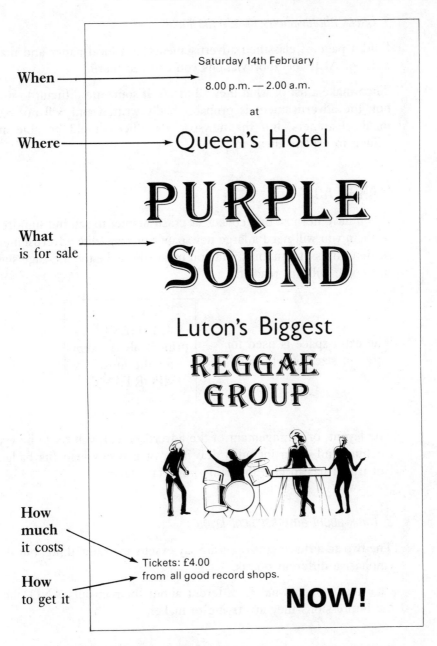

Saturday 14th February

8.00 p.m. — 2.00 a.m.

at

Queen's Hotel

PURPLE
SOUND

Luton's Biggest

REGGAE
GROUP

Tickets: £4.00
from all good record shops.

NOW!

To save money, classified advertisements are usually **very short** and **use abbreviations**, like these:

v.g.c.	*instead of*	in very good condition;
£40 o.n.o.	*instead of*	£40 or near offer;
2 recep, 3 beds	*instead of*	two 'reception' rooms and 3 bedrooms.

1 Check abbreviations in advertisements

Find a page of classified advertisements in a local paper and make a list of ALL the abbreviations you can see there.

Then make a list of what they all mean. If some are difficult to work out, the advertisement is probably badly written and will not have many customers, but the newspaper's office should be able and willing to explain these to you.

'LARGE ADS'

If you have not just one cooker or crash helmet to sell but hundreds of them you will need a large newspaper or magazine advertisement, or thousands of handbills, but you must still make the message short or people will not read it.

The extra space is used for different sizes of lettering

> The
> LARGEST
> print is always kept
> for the most
> IMPORTANT
> words.

The layout, or arrangement of the advertisement, will try to be eye-catching and often includes drawings, or a firm's logo (its badge). But it still has to give the same important facts.

2 Think about advertisement layout

The two advertisements opposite say exactly the same thing, but they emphasise different points.

Can you explain what is different about their layouts AND about the impressions they are trying to make?

An advertisement has to persuade you to try something, whether that 'something' is a special church service or a nail varnish made from gold dust. So it needs to:

> catch your attention
> *and*
> convince you that what it has to offer is worth trying.

In their pictures, advertisers use gorgeous colours, attractive men and women, beautiful houses, luxury cars, even clean children and well-behaved pets, all to make you look and listen.

In their words, advertisers use language which does FOUR jobs:

- it sounds simple
- it sounds luxurious
- it sounds urgent
- it stresses every point except (of course) the high price

3 Sales talk

Look at these examples of sales talk. How many of the FOUR language jobs is done by each one?

- Looks a million dollars — but costs only £2 a week!
- Send NO MONEY now.
- 12 MONTHS to pay.
- Buy NOW and SAVE £60!
- Send TODAY for our FREE brochure.
- Order on FREEphone 09 327 2121.
- It's so EASY — just fill in this coupon.
- Superb craftsmanship, exclusive designs.
- Uses the best leather/oak/silk/gem stones.
- Bargain Offer! 4 LUXURY towels for the price of 3.
- Hurry! Order NOW while stocks last!
- Buy TODAY and have a chance of winning FIRST PRIZE in our free MILLION POUND competition!

4 Think why advertisements work

Look for SIX leaflets or magazine advertisements, for SIX different products, which you think are good at catching your attention and at making you want to try the product.

Then decide what it is that makes each one so good. Is it the large print, the drawings, the layout — or a special gimmick?

5 Television advertising

Describe to a friend two television advertisements, one which you think works and one which fails.

Discuss how:
    words,
    music,
    people,
    animals,
    special effects,
make one advertisement so much better than the other.

BROCHURES, CATALOGUES AND TIMETABLES

Glossy mail-order catalogues and travel brochures are full of tempting colour pictures. They make us want what is on offer. But what will it cost? The price can be hard to work out because it is often hidden in a complicated table with lots of columns.

When you have several columns to sort out, **look first at the headings in the top row** to check what kinds of information the table can give you.

Next look at the column on the left hand side: the basic facts are usually listed there.

6 Use a table from a travel brochure

This table is one to daydream about:

REGION	Pages	Special Rates for Groups of 6 or more	NO Single Room Supplement	Free Water Sports	Manchester OR London departures available	Special Rates for Business People
MIDDLE & FAR EAST						
Bali	12–14		■	■	■	■
Delhi	15–17	■	■			■
Hong Kong	18–20			■		■
Malaysia	21–22	■	■		■	■
Pakistan	23–25	■	■			■
Singapore	26			■		■
Sri Lanka	27–28	■	■	■	■	■
Thailand	29–30	■		■	■	■

a) Work out which holiday resort in this table seems the best bargain for a family of seven from the north of England. (The *basic* holiday price is the same for each of the eight countries.) The family includes:

> three teenagers (two girls and one boy),
> their parents,
> their uncle,
> their grandmother.

All of them are sailing or waterski champions.

b) Explain why you think the resort is such a bargain.

c) Judging again from this brochure's offers, work out which holiday resort of the eight listed seems most keen to attract visitors.

d) Which kind of visitor seems most welcome in all of these resorts?

e) Working in pairs, collect a free travel brochure for any ONE of the eight places listed.
Find out all you can from the brochure about the place you choose. For example:

> the cheapest and dearest times to go there;
> how long the flying time is from London or from
>   Manchester;
> the temperatures in August and in January;
> the kinds of day trips you could make when you are there;
> which hotel you would like to stay at, and why.

Check in an atlas where your chosen resort is.
Then, working with your partner, explain to others in your group what your chosen holiday and hotel have to offer. **Try to convince them that your chosen holiday is the best one.**

f) Write a description of the place you would choose to visit — one of these eight or somewhere else — giving your reasons.
Assume you could afford to go anywhere in the world, and write at least 100 words (using one or two paragraphs) but not more than 500 (about five paragraphs).

7 Use a catalogue

Collect two or three trade or mail-order catalogues and at least one order form for each catalogue. (Large electrical shops or Do-It-Yourself stores will usually supply them free.)

Look at those pages in each catalogue which deal with ONE particular item you would like to buy, whether it is a new jacket, a television set, hi-fi equipment or a new bike.

Compare the information the catalogues give about the different makes and models available. Then make a shortlist of THREE rival products you would choose from if you were going to buy one.

Make a note of:

> the price of each of the three;
> which catalogue it is in, and the page number;
> the make and style;
> the catalogue or reference number;
> the size;
> special features.

If you are working with other students, tell them about the facts you have shortlisted, showing them the catalogues. Discuss which model is likely to suit you *and* what you can afford to pay.

If you are working on your own *or* in a group, write one paragraph about the make you think would suit you best.

8 Fill in a catalogue order form

Your family wants to order some Christmas presents from a mail-order catalogue and has left you to fill in the order form.

Use one of the order forms you collected for exercise 7 OR copy out the form printed on page 44; then fill in the details of your order, sorting these out from this rough list:

1 From page 63, a navy (or dark blue) handbag, with shoulder strap, Catalogue Number BKH 370, @ £9.59.

2 From page 194, two boxes of pink Fragrant Cloud soaps, at £1.99 each. (Second choice blue.) Catalogue No. BKIT3970. (Total cost = £3.98.)

3 Man's imitation leather bomber jacket, 42″ chest, Cat. No. BKL293 @ £21.99, see page 36. Dark grey or white.

4 Catalogue number BKM303303, page 79, man's polo neck sweater, 46 inch chest. Costs £16.99. Must be black.

5 Fair Dinkum toy koala bear, on page 3. Costs £7.49 for the 18 inch one. Cat. No. BKCT49(b).

Bees Knees Mail Order Co. plc

30–36 Dynevor Street, Barry, West Glamorgan
(0446) 231231–4

ORDER FORM

Please use Block Capitals

Quantity	Item	Size	Brand Name or Style	Colour		Catalogue No.	Page No.	Price of Item	Total Price
				First choice	Second choice				

Name: _____

Address: _____

_____

Tel. No.: _____

Please state month when delivery is required: _____
(Goods will be despatched on 18th of month selected)

Method of payment: Cheque enclosed / Monthly payments /
Cash on delivery

(Please delete as necessary)

Signature: _____

Date of order: _____

9 Collect a timetable

Collect a free local bus timetable from your nearest bus station. Working *either* on your own *or* with a partner, write down your answers to these questions.

a) What is the shortest and what is the longest journey it gives the times for?

b) What are the differences between the bus services for weekdays, Saturdays and Sundays?

c) Why do you think bus (and train) timetables use a '24-hour clock' instead of the 12-hour one we use normally?

d) Use the bus timetable *and* your own experience of local buses to make TWO lists.
   In one write all the good points about local bus services and in the other put all the bad points about them. Write about things like:
   how frequently the buses run
   fares
   cleanliness of buses and bus shelters
   helpfulness of drivers and other staff
   the local bus station
   Arrange the lists you write in two columns, side by side. Which list is longer?

10 Use a timetable

Using your local timetable, plan a day trip.

It could be to a sports event, a concert or a shopping centre, for example.

If you need to check, look in the 'What's On' column of the local paper, or ask for information at the library or bus station.

a) Make a plan for the day, listing:
   the time to leave home
   the time the bus leaves
   the time the bus will get there
   the time the place you are visiting will open
   the time it will close (or you will have to leave)
   the time of the best bus home AND (in case you miss it)
      of the next one
   the time you expect to reach home

b) If you are able to, make the day trip you have planned.
Then write TWO advertisements, based on your day out:

     write one for the bus company
     write the other for the place or event you have visited

Mention only the good points.

c) Discuss with other students the good *and* the bad points about
your day out.

2 Reading on your own

NEWSPAPERS

Newspapers try to do several of the things an advertisement does:

     say a lot in a little space;
     be easy to understand;
     persuade us that what they say is right.

National papers try to tell us the truth about every important event
in the world since the paper was last printed. Even local papers try
to cover everything of interest in the area, from cat shows to car
thefts.

Of course they are trying to do the impossible. What they do is tell
you what reporters think about the stories the **editor** believes are
important.

One local paper may use the opening of a new supermarket as its
front page story, while another chooses the visit of a politician or
a pop star's poodle.

11 Check the news

Look at any TWO national newspapers (not local ones) printed on
the same day, and check the following points:

a) Are their front page (or 'leading') articles about the same news
item? If not, which paper do you think has chosen the more
important story for its leading article?

Is the front page story of one paper printed on a less important page in the other?

b) If the same story is covered, somewhere, by both papers, are the facts and ideas they give you:

the same?
almost the same?
obviously different?

12 Check the news

Looking at the same two papers, check these points:

- how many pages does each one have?
- what kinds of things are the back page stories about?
- how many complete pages do you think are used up by advertisements in each paper?
- how many pages worth of space seem to be used up, in each paper, for national or foreign news stories which you think are really important?
- what other features are there apart from national or foreign news stories? For example:

Births, Marriages and Deaths announcements
cartoons
crosswords
fashion
'glamour' pictures
horoscopes
reviews of records, films, videos, plays or books
television programme guides
weather maps

How much space do they have, compared with the news stories?

Using what you have just found out, write 100 words on the differences between the two papers.

LAYOUT

The layout of a news story is important too, not just which page it appears on.

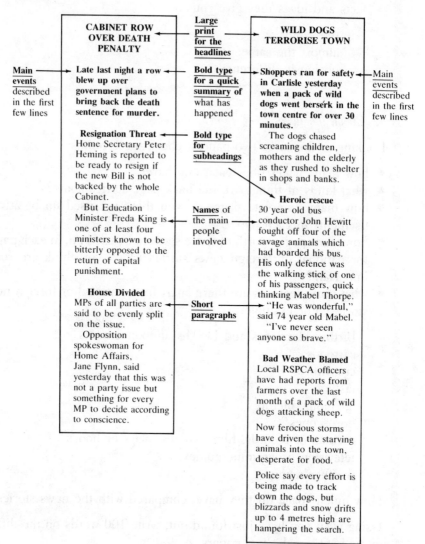

CABINET ROW OVER DEATH PENALTY

Main events described in the first few lines

Large print for the headlines

Late last night a row blew up over government plans to bring back the death sentence for murder.

Bold type for a quick summary of what has happened

Resignation Threat
Home Secretary Peter Heming is reported to be ready to resign if the new Bill is not backed by the whole Cabinet.
But Education Minister Freda King is one of at least four ministers known to be bitterly opposed to the return of capital punishment.

Bold type for subheadings

Names of the main people involved

House Divided
MPs of all parties are said to be evenly split on the issue.
Opposition spokeswoman for Home Affairs, Jane Flynn, said yesterday that this was not a party issue but something for every MP to decide according to conscience.

Short paragraphs

WILD DOGS TERRORISE TOWN

Shoppers ran for safety in Carlisle yesterday when a pack of wild dogs went berserk in the town centre for over 30 minutes.
The dogs chased screaming children, mothers and the elderly as they rushed to shelter in shops and banks.

Main events described in the first few lines

Heroic rescue
30 year old bus conductor John Hewitt fought off four of the savage animals which had boarded his bus. His only defence was the walking stick of one of his passengers, quick thinking Mabel Thorpe.
"He was wonderful," said 74 year old Mabel. "I've never seen anyone so brave."

Bad Weather Blamed
Local RSPCA officers have had reports from farmers over the last month of a pack of wild dogs attacking sheep.

Now ferocious storms have driven the starving animals into the town, desperate for food.

Police say every effort is being made to track down the dogs, but blizzards and snow drifts up to 4 metres high are hampering the search.

Newspaper stories have to pack a lot of information into a short space. There was no room for the 'Wild Dogs' article to explain the initials RSPCA, and the 'Cabinet Row' report expected you to understand a few of the technical terms of politics — for example 'Bill' and 'Cabinet'.

13 Technical terms

Look up these technical terms in a dictionary or encyclopaedia:

Cabinet
Home Secretary
House of Commons
House of Lords
Opposition
Act of Parliament
Bill
Capital punishment

If some of these are hard to find, librarians are usually pleased to help anyone hunting for information.

Children's encyclopaedias are often the best place to start looking for information. This is because they give you intelligent explanations but do not expect you to know anything very technical.

14 Find out what the papers say

Read the leading, front page article in your most recent local paper — one that your friends or fellow students are not likely to have seen yet.

Then explain to them, as simply and briefly as you can, what the article is about AND discuss your views on it with them.

15 Discuss

Discuss one of the following topics with a small group of friends or with other students in your group, after finding out as much information as you can about it.

Should there be capital punishment for certain crimes?
Why do we need Members of Parliament?
Why do people read newspapers?

BOOKS, FILMS AND PLAYS

A newspaper article tells you right at the start the main point of the story.

Most books, films and plays do the opposite. They keep you guessing about what will happen until you are only five minutes from the end.

You get clues about what will happen, though sometimes these are false clues, making you guess wrongly, so that the ending is more of a surprise.

16 Follow the clues

See what you can work out about this extract from a short story.

> Suddenly he stumbled on a stone. Righting himself he peered ahead, straining his eyes to make out what was in front of him in the darkness. He was always glad when this bit of the road was over.
>
> His face and ears tingled in the cold, fine rain. Sodden branches dripped heavily on his shoulders and the dense trees seemed to grow even thicker and closer together, becoming huge black shapes, threatening him.
>
> He tried not to look into the black depths on each side, tried not to think of who or what might be hiding there, watching, waiting for him to stumble again, to fall, to lie there helpless. If anything happened to him here, there would be no chance of help, no one would find him for weeks.

Working on your own or with a small group, **read this extract again**, then:

- list all the facts you can gather from it
- decide who the character is (make up his name, age, height, nationality, family)
- decide where he is
- decide why, and when, he is there
- decide what you think will happen to him next
- work out how the story could end.

Write down all the things you have decided on, *either* in a list *or* in one or two short paragraphs.

Then, if you are working with a group of people, explain your ideas about the man and what is happening to him.

Compare your ideas with other people's. The more different ideas, or 'plots', you can all invent the better.

Lastly, choose ONE of the plots you have now talked about and write the story. Decide the length for yourself, but it should be at least 150 words.

17 Follow the clues

Repeat ALL the steps of the last exercise, using an extract taken from any book or video film you have a copy of, but have not read or seen all the way through.

Choose a piece from about half way through, because here the events should be happening faster, but you will not know how the plot begins or ends.

3 Write it out yourself

18 Write a classified advertisement

You want to sell your old snooker table and buy a new one. The one you want to sell is a bit scratched but the slate is good and the green baize cover is in good condition. It is 3.66 metres long and 1.86 metres wide. You would like to get £80 for it but would take £70 if you couldn't do any better.

Write a classified advertisement for the table, making it as brief as you can, but remember to include all the necessary facts (**what, where, when, how much**).

19 Write a shop window advertisement

Write a brief advertisement for any secondhand goods you choose, OR for a window cleaning business you are trying to start up.
Your advertisement is to go in a newsagent's window.

20 Newspaper advertisement

Photocopy or copy out the form opposite, taken from the *Christchurch Chronicle*. Then complete it, making up an advertisement for any item which fits one of the eight different groups mentioned.

21 Write a leaflet

Write a leaflet advertising a jumble sale OR a car boot sale. Use layout and different sized lettering to emphasise some headings more than others.

22 Design a poster

Draw up a poster for an important concert to be held in aid of a local charity.

Make up the date, time, place and the names of at least THREE bands who will appear in the programme.

23 Fill in an order form

Using any mail-order catalogue (and order form) you choose:

- decide on THREE items you would like to order, regardless of cost
- list all the necessary details (including the catalogue number, make, type, size, colour and materials, wherever these are necessary).
- fill in the firm's order form, giving all the information it asks for
- check the catalogue AND your notes to make sure you have given all the right facts

24 Book a holiday

Ask for a free holiday brochure and booking form at a travel agent's, or at your nearest Tourist Information Centre (your library or telephone directory will help you find its address). Choose a holiday from the brochure.
Work out:

- where you will go
- which hotel to book

CHRISTCHURCH CHRONICLE
FAST SALE ADS

ONLY 25p per word inc. VAT

Use this coupon for any article you want to buy or sell for over £50.

Write one word in each space provided (including your address or telephone number):

1	2	3	4
5	6	7	8
9	10	11	12
13	14	15	16
17	18	19	20

- The publishers reserve the right to alter or omit any advertisement without consulting the advertiser.
- The deadline is 1.00 p.m. Wednesday.
- No advertisements may be made on this coupon for animals, cars, motorcycles or caravans.
- Please tick the appropriate category:

1 Electrical		5 TV or Hi-fi	
2 Furniture		6 Toys	
3 Gardening		7 Miscellaneous	
4 Sports goods		8 Goods wanted	

I have enclosed CHEQUE/POSTAL ORDER No: _____

for (please state amount): £ _____

Signed: _____

Name: _____

Address: _____

_____

Tel. No: _____ Date: _____

Post your completed coupon to CHRONICLE FAST SALE ADS, HERON ROAD, CHRISTCHURCH

- who will come with you
- the meals to book: bed and breakfast
  or half board (breakfast + 1 main meal)
  or full board (breakfast + lunch + evening meal);
- when your holiday will start
- any special arrangements (single/double rooms/sea view and balcony/private bathroom/. . .)
- the insurance needed (for how many days; for accident only *or* for accident + medical expenses + loss of baggage)
- the cost per person

When you have decided on all of these, fill in the booking form OR make a list of all the arrangements you have chosen and include the holiday reference number given in the brochure.

25 Write a newspaper article

Write a short article, between 100 and 200 words long, for a local paper OR for your newsletter at college or at work, about a local event which has just been held. For example:

    a sports event
    a carnival, flower show or pet show
    a circus
    a strike or 'sit in'
    a fire or road accident
    an amateur play or musical
    a fashion show
    a concert

26 Describe a character

Choose a television programme which you enjoy. Describe to a friend ONE of the characters in the programme. Then write out your description, using at least 100 words.

27 Finish the story

The story so far . . .

Fifteen years ago a man came to work in Britain, bringing his wife and his son and daughter. A year later they had another child.

Now the man's father has died abroad and left a prosperous business to his son. The man and his wife want to return to their native country and run the business, leaving Britain for good. The children, now aged 19, 17 and 14 want to stay.

Discuss the different ideas and feelings you think these five people would have.

Then write as if you were one of the five people writing to a close friend, explaining what has happened and how you feel about it. Make up all the names and place names you need, and write at least 100 words.

The parents can come from any country you choose, except Britain.

4 Words: housing

Getting our own place to live is harder for many of us than it was for this young man and his wife, but even for him it was not easy. Read what he has to say about it.

Somewhere to Live

Our first home was really just a bedsitting room, though the landlord called it a basement flat. We shared the bathroom and the kitchen was really a sort of a cupboard, partitioned off from what had once been the cellar of the three storey Victorian semi-detached barn of a place.

Of course Vita's parents said we'd be better off in their spare bedroom. They didn't want any rent, so our only expenditure would be on food and our share of the rates and fuel bills. We knew we could economise if we moved in with them: we were trying hard to save up for a deposit on a house of our own and, besides, furniture costs money. We didn't want to get a place of our own and camp there, using every penny we earned to pay the mortgage and hire purchase bills every month.

So we tried it. We moved in just after our second wedding anniversary and their thirtieth, and we saved about twenty-five pounds a week, on average. But it didn't work.

I couldn't cope with my in-laws breathing down our necks and Vita was fed up with sharing the kitchen before the first week was out. There wasn't much chance of privacy for them or for us in a modern bungalow with plasterboard walls and one bathroom, six feet by seven. Even the dustbin was overcrowded!

We all tried hard, but Vita's parents were so relieved when we said we'd seen a little house we liked that we almost had a party — it was the best evening we'd had together since we'd moved in.

The house was on the new housing development at Lodge Farm and was no mansion. We'd hoped for something a bit bigger than a two-up, one-down terraced house with bathroom and kitchen, but we shopped around a bit and got a 90% mortage from one of the big building societies and we had very nice neighbours. In twenty-five years our starter home would all be ours!

Now for just a few thousand more, we have this superb detached residence

28 Check the meaning

Check the meanings of ALL the words and phrases which are underlined in the 'Somewhere to Live' passage.

Discuss the good and bad points of the three homes this young couple had.

Lastly, write down your ideas about them, using one paragraph for your views on each of their three homes.

29 Find the information

Read the following chart carefully.

Column 1	Column 2
Estate agent's office	The cheapest houses, flats and bungalows for sale in your area, freehold and leasehold How much it costs to rent a flat, house or bedsitting room.
Council's Housing Department	Council houses and flats The waiting list: — how to join it — how many people are on it — what kinds of people join it — how long people usually wait before being housed How high rents are Which districts council housing is in
Building society or bank	How to apply for a mortgage How old you have to be to apply How much deposit people have to pay How long you can take to pay the mortgage How much it costs to borrow money

Visit ONE of the places in Column 1 and find out all you can from the staff there about the points linked to it in Column 2.

Collect useful leaflets and make a note of all the facts you are given.

30 Report your findings

Look through all the leaflets and notes you collected when you did exercise 29.

Then explain to the other students in your group what you have found out. Listen to what others have found out on their visits.

Discuss the kind of house or flat you would like best, and how to go about finding somewhere to live.

5 How to set it out: paragraphs

To make what you write easy for people to take in, split it up into paragraphs.

The title goes here ———→ **FASHION**

Each paragraph begins on a new line, about 3 centimetres from the margin.

(3 cm) Paragraph one will explain the rough idea of whatever you are writing about. Often paragraph one is quite short, because it just has to **start things off**.

Every paragraph should normally be at least two lines long.

Every page of writing must have **at least one new paragraph**.

(3 cm) Paragraph two will usually be about one out of many of the things covered by the title. On 'Fashion' you could write here about **fashions in ancient times**, like Roman togas and Egyptian jewellery. When you finished with ancient fashion, then you would finish your paragraph.

The **average** length of a paragraph is about six to ten lines (shorter in a business letter, or a newspaper article).

Start a new paragraph when you write about a different idea, a different mood or a different person.

(3 cm) Now you could write about **fashions in recent times**, from crinolines to denim jeans and punk safety pins, describing these different examples and explaining when people wore them.

(3 cm) When you wanted to write about **fashions in other things besides clothes**, you would have to start a new paragraph again of course.

Your last paragraph should *not* include new ideas or examples. Use it to sum up your ideas.

On 'Fashion' you could end like this:

So hairstyles and hemlines may change — but be warned. Don't throw out those flares and minis.
   The clothes which looked great yesterday, and gruesome today, will be gorgeous again tomorrow.

31 Put in paragraphs and capital letters

The layout of the next piece of writing is bad, because it is all lumped together in one paragraph. Four capital letters are missing as well.

Read it through AT LEAST TWICE. Then copy it out, using a new paragraph when you think one is needed **because something different is being written about**. Put in the missing capital letters too.

My Ideal Home

When I was six, my ideal home would have had at least three puppies, no ghosts on the stairs, my favourite china doll and a low bathroom sink. Ordinary sinks were hard to reach. At hair-washing times that meant soggy pyjamas, eyes full of soapy water, a flooded bathroom floor when I struggled to get away, and half an hour of tears — mine and my mother's. By fourteen I had changed my ideas. It was a pale pink bedroom with a frilled nylon bedspread that i wanted now, a four poster, and as many cages full of canaries as possible. The last idea came from a book I read just then about a good and beautiful rich young girl, living in a mansion, whose father gave her a dozen golden birdcages, each with two golden canaries inside. I think at the time I somehow felt that a few canaries would make me good and beautiful and rich too. I went on living in a Victorian semi-detached and never got the canaries, so I shall never know if they would have worked. When I was a bachelor girl earning my own living, I got a base-ment flat. Then I found out about the cost of rent and rates, that carpets seem to cost half a year's wages, and that it's a mistake to buy a small cooker. It may be big enough to cook spaghetti on toast, but hungry friends and neighbours expect proper meals: proper meals need four burners and a decent sized oven, or else a flat with an indian take-away on one side and a chinese on the other. Now I am older I know what an ideal home really is. It is one where the central heating never breaks down, the mortgage is a small one, the plumbing never leaks, the television is never struck by lightning in the middle of 'dynasty', and neither the cat nor your family ever comes in with mud on its paws.

32 Write a description

Make a list of all the words used in 'My Ideal Home' which were used and underlined in 'Somewhere to Live' (see pages 55–56).

Then write a description called 'The Place Where I Live' and include each of the words in your list.

33 Write in paragraphs

Discuss what an ideal home would be like. Then write down your ideas, using at least two paragraphs.

6 Get it right: 'them' and 'those'

You like | them | don't you?

or

You like | those | don't you?

or

You like | those | new cars don't you?

1 **Them** has to be a lonely word, working on its own with no other word to partner it:

I bought **them** from the Oxfam shop.

NEVER say 'them things' or 'them people' or 'them places'. ALWAYS say just '**them**'.

<u>EXAMPLES</u>

I saw **them** running away from the van as it burst into flames. Didn't you see **them** in the sale, at half the price you paid last week?

2 **Those** can work on its own:

How much did **those** cost?

OR it can be paired off with another word if you want to make it really clear what you are talking about:

How much did **those boots** cost?

<u>EXAMPLES</u>

I gave you **those** half an hour ago.

OR

I gave you **those cassettes** half an hour ago.

What are **those** doing in the fridge?

OR

What are **those striped pyjamas** doing in the fridge?

34 Use THOSE and THEM

Write three sentences, each using the word **those**.

Write another three sentences, each using the word **them**.

UNIT THREE

SORT OUT YOUR IDEAS

SORT OUT YOUR IDEAS

1 Put things in order

When you are looking for information, and when you are storing it away for future use, you have to understand the main ways of arranging it:

alphabetical order
date order
age order
number order
rank order

The telephone directory for your area lists all people with telephones, in alphabetical order according to the names of their families or firms.

If several people have the same family name, they will be listed in order of their other names — like Daljit, David, P.J. or Riley:

Pilt Daljit, 16 Dynevor Drive, Duston	....	Colchester 16699
Pilt David, 32 Ardleigh Avenue	....	Dedham 43210
Pilt P.J., 2 Copdock Road	....	Copford 22311
Pilt and Riley, Mkt Gdners, End Lane	....	Goldhanger 91199

1 Put names in alphabetical order

Fifteen new people with telephones have to be included under the letter D in the new directory for your area. Their names are listed here in the wrong order.

Using the same heading, write out the list again, putting it in alphabetical order.

Then give each name a new number, from 1 to 15, according to its place in the list.

NEW TELEPHONE SUBSCRIBERS

1 Donowicz J.F.
2 Dunwoody J, Carpenter & Joiner
3 Diamond Freezer Co.
4 Dampcure Timber Treatment
5 Duong Lee Tam
6 Del Greco A.
7 Di Giorgio R.

8 Dairy Fresh Foods
9 Danvers-Colquhoun R.N.
10 Di Carlo J.L.
11 Diamond L.T.
12 Darji M.
13 Dibworth M.
14 Duo Dating Agency
15 Defence, Ministry of

■ ADVICE
▬▬▬

1 Find all the names beginning with DA (there are four).
Copy them out in the order in which you find them.
Don't worry about the other letters in the names yet.

2 Then look at the THIRD letter of each one, and **number** the names in their proper order.
For example, number all the names beginning with DA in alphabetical order according to the THIRD letter in each name (so that Dairy comes before Dampcure).

3 Now look for names beginning with DB, then DC, and so on through the alphabet, until you come to the name which has to go next in your list.

4 Lastly, write out the whole list again, this time in the **new** number order, from 1 to 15.

---

2 List names in alphabetical order

Write down the names of twenty shops and other firms in your area.

Then write out the list again, putting all the names in alphabetical order. Number them from 1 to 20. Head your list LOCAL FIRMS.

3 List people in age order

These ten children all have to have injections against tetanus and polio when they are five years old.

Write out their names and dates of birth again so that they are in age order. Start with the oldest child's name and date of birth and end with the youngest one's.

Use three columns, and the same headings, as in this printed list:

NUMBER	NAME	DATE OF BIRTH
1	Abbott, Gregory	5 October 1987
2	Constaninou, Demetrios	12 February 1989
3	Exeter, Ann	17 March 1991
4	Fernando, Anton	1 May 1988
5	Glenisla, Fraser	4 November 1989
6	Masih, Joseph	17 June 1987
7	Montague, Delphine	20 June 1989
8	Pearlman, Leroy	23 April 1988
9	Rasta, Diana	18 December 1989
10	Xavala, Carlos	9 January 1990

■ ADVICE

1 **This time deal with one YEAR at a time.**
Begin with 1987.
Write out the names and dates of children born in 1987, in the order you find them in (there are two).

2 **Number** these two in the order in which they were born.

3 Then write out the names and dates of the two children born in 1988. Number these 3 and 4, in age order — elder one first.

4 Do the same for the rest of the children. Work on one year at a time.

5 Lastly, write out your list again, **in the order of the NEW numbers**, from 1 to 10.

4 Put people in age order

Write down the names and dates of birth of twelve friends and relatives OR of twelve famous people. Then write out your list of names and dates again, in age order. Put the youngest first this time, and end with the oldest.

List the names and dates in two columns, with the dates on the right, and number the names from 1 to 12.

Use the same headings as you did in the last exercise.

5 List firms according to size

The following list of firms is in alphabetical order.
Write it out in a different order, according to the TOTAL number of staff employed by each firm. (Do *not* list male and female staff separately.)

Begin the list with the firm which has the most staff and end with the firm which has the fewest.

Use three main columns: one headed FIRMS, and one on the right headed TOTAL NUMBER OF STAFF. Then number the firms from 1 to 10, in a separate column on the left.

| NUMBER | FIRMS | EMPLOYEES | | ANNUAL TURNOVER |
		men	women	in £s (thousands)
1	A to Z Safety Agency	10	15	293
2	Betteridge Roofing Supplies	58	29	1,003
3	Caribbean Shipping Company	15	12	391
4	Decortex Industrial Paints	537	293	8,810
5	Freckles Cosmetics	215	372	6,203
6	Golden Spanner Garages	53	6	636
7	Happy Sprat Fish Packers	115	190	2,520
8	Kopy Kat Printers	19	29	305
9	Mole Control	3	1	39
10	Tandem Truck & Car Hire	5	7	112

■ ADVICE

1 Add up the number of male and female employees at each firm. Write the total next to the name of the firm.

2 Now write the totals for all ten firms in a new list, in a column on the right of the page. Start with the largest number and work down in order of size, so that the smallest number comes last.

3 Now add the names of the firms, in a column on the left, writing each one next to the total number of people it employs.

4 Lastly, number the new list from 1 to 10 in the left-hand margin.

6 List firms according to annual turnover

Look again at the list of firms given on page 65. Write the list out again: this time arrange the firms according to the size of their annual turnover (or yearly income). Start with the firm with the largest annual turnover.

Use two columns: one on the left headed FIRMS, and one on the right headed ANNUAL TURNOVER.

Then number the firms from 1 to 10, in the margin on the left.

7 Put things in rank order AND order of cost

Write down the names of 15 luxury items you think the perfect home should have.

Now write them out again, listing them in order of their importance to you, starting with the best one (that is, in **rank** order).

Then find out the cost of each item and make a new list, this time according to how much the items **cost**, starting with the most expensive one.

If you find this task useful practice, you can repeat it, listing 15 other items in order of your preference, then in order of their cost. You could list:

cars or motorbikes   plants for a garden
magazines   package holidays
sports equipment   cassettes or compact discs

8 Write out a route

Your sister has to drive from Handsworth in Birmingham to Worcester. The trouble is that, on the way there, she has to collect a friend from Dudley *and* then deliver a wedding present to a cousin in Upton Snodsbury.

She does *not* know the way.

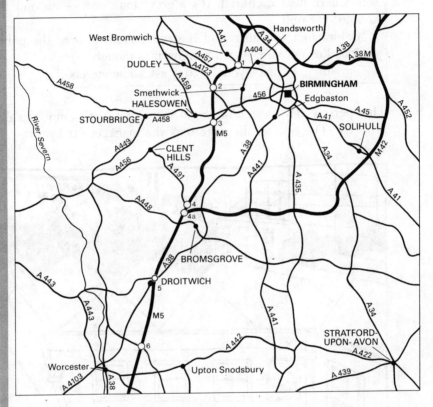

Look at the map printed above, and find the way your sister will have to drive.

Then make a list of the reference numbers of all the roads she will take. **List them in order for her.** Now write out a numbered list of directions for your sister. Include the name of the town each road leads to. Use the heading:

ROUTE FROM HANDSWORTH TO DUDLEY, UPTON SNODSBURY AND WORCESTER

Start your list with this line:

1 Take the A4040 towards West Bromwich.

2 How to give instructions

'The new Sure-Fit factory? Oh dear!

'Well, you turn left here and then drive straight on —

'How far? About a mile I think, then you have to turn by a pub, somewhere near a church. It's a grey stone one — no, not the church, the pub.

'Before that you go round the roundabout next to the police station. I'm not sure which turning it is though.

'I'm sorry. Perhaps you'd better ask someone else.'

That person may *know* how to get there, but just cannot explain it properly. The one on the page opposite manages far better!

'But the bloke said third left, opposite the corner pub.'

'The new Sure-Fit factory? Yes, I know where it is.

'Take the next turning on the left and drive straight on till you come to a roundabout. There's a big police station on the left just there. You can't miss it.

'Take the third turning off the roundabout and you'll be in Devon Road, with the Plaza Cinema on your left.

'Go straight on for about five blocks: on the right you'll pass a pub called The Moot Meet and a new church.

'Then turn left at the traffic lights, into Button Lane.

'The factory is about a mile further on, on the right, opposite the Shessaco Garage.'

9 Why some instructions work better than others

The first set of instructions would probably have you lost inside ten minutes.

Work out three reasons to explain WHY the second set is better.

When you give instructions, whether they are on securing a load on a ten ton truck or on shampooing a hamster, you will probably have to teach people how to cope, alone, with jobs they have never even tried before.

As you explain what to do, imagine that you are going through all the stages of the job yourself:

use **simple** words
in **short** sentences
to explain **one step** at a time
in the **right** order
with **checkpoints** to watch out for, to show that all is well.

If you write the instructions down, make them easy to read:

put them in a **list**;
give each step a **number**;
use **wide margins**;
leave a two-line **space** between each step;
give the whole thing a **simple heading**.

10 Put instructions in the right order

Write the following instructions out again, putting them in a **sensible order**. The diagram should make this easier to do.

Then number each point, in its new order.

There is no need to change the words.

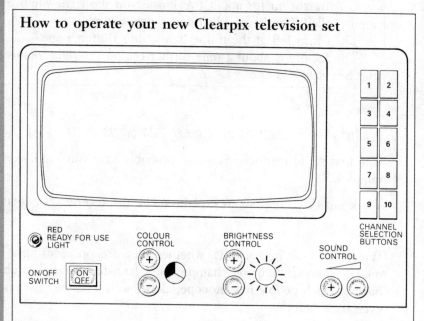

How to operate your new Clearpix television set

The pair next to the symbol ◐ will alter the colour of the picture.

The pair next to the symbol ☼ will alter the brightness of the picture.

The pair next to the symbol ◁ will alter the sound volume.

To switch off the set, press the [ON/OFF] button once more.

The red Ready-for-Use light next to the button will then come on.

Press the Channel Selection button which has the number of the channel you want to watch.

In each pair one button is marked ⊖ . Press this to **decrease** colour, brightness or sound.

Plug the television cable into a power socket and switch on the power supply.

The other button is marked (+). Press this to **increase** colour, brightness or sound.

There is a separate Channel Selection button for each channel, on the right of the switch panel.

There are six more buttons on the switch panel, in the middle. They are arranged in three pairs.

Then switch on the set by pressing the ⎡ON OFF⎤ button at the bottom of the set, on the left of the switch panel.
The red Ready-for-Use light next to the button will then come on.

11 Make a clear list of instructions

The following instructions on how to park a car are *not* helpful:

- they are not in a list
- the steps are in the wrong order
- some explanations need to be made clearer

How to park a car

When you want to park a car you have to press the brake pedal and find a parking space large enough. When you stop you should leave the gears in the neutral position and switch off the engine.

Of course you have to change down to a low gear before you stop.

Before you slow down you should indicate that you are going to go left or right, and before that you should have looked in your mirror. This is to make sure nothing is driving so close behind you and so fast that it might hit your car if you slow down too soon.

Write the instructions out again, in the right order, in a numbered list.

Make them easy to read *and* easy to follow. Change some of the words if that would help.

Use the same heading.

3 How to get it down on paper

How you describe something depends on:

what you are describing;
who will read it; *and*
why.

'Not new, but only one careful female owner' would be fine to describe a secondhand car in the Classified Advertisements, though it would be a bit unusual to describe your father like that.

But the trouble with most descriptions is what they leave out, *not* what they put in.

Think about these two:

> This creature is wild, pale grey and can run fast. When it is disturbed it often gives a high pitched alarm call.

AND

> This famous person is very intelligent, respected, thoughtful, travels a lot and almost always wears a hat in public.

The first description could be of any one of a hundred creatures, from a mouse to a monkey. Even an elephant is possible.

The second one could be about almost anyone, from the Queen of England to the Pope or Elton John.

When you write a description:
- decide what people **need to know;**
- write all this down in a **list;**
- **number** the points in your list in order of importance, with the main one first;
- then write out all this again **using proper sentences and paragraphs**, in the order of your numbered points.

HOW TO DESCRIBE PEOPLE

Your description of yourself for a pen friend would include a lot about your personality, appearance and social life.

The description you give when you apply for a job has to be much

CURRICULUM VITAE

1 **NAME** (underline your FAMILY NAME)
2 **TITLE** (MR/MRS/MISS/MS/DR)
3 **DATE OF BIRTH** (DAY + MONTH + YEAR, in numbers)
4 **MARITAL STATUS** (SINGLE/MARRIED/DIVORCED)
5 **SCHOOLS ATTENDED**

DATES		NAMES OF SCHOOLS
FROM	*TO*	
		(Give them in the order in which you attended them.)

6 **QUALIFICATIONS**

EXAMINATION	SUBJECTS	YEAR TAKEN	GRADE ACHIEVED

7 **EMPLOYMENT**

EMPLOYER	POSITION HELD	DATES
(List: full time jobs part time jobs placements voluntary work)		

8 **HOBBIES & INTERESTS**

(List the most important ones first — especially the ones useful to your work such as:
    weight training, speaking a second language, first aid)

9 **OTHER INFORMATION**

For example: can you drive a car/tractor/van?
              would you be willing to retrain or move?
              are you taking any courses now?

more factual. Often a firm will ask you to write your curriculum vitae or 'c.v.' for them. This is a list of facts, about you and your life so far, given under headings like the ones used on page 73.

(See also Unit 4 pages 94–98.)

The headings should always use BLOCK CAPITALS. You do not have to number them but they do look neater that way.

If you apply for a lot of jobs, you can photocopy your c.v. and send a copy of the same one every time you apply for a job, until it is out of date. So writing or typing a really neat one will save you a lot of time and trouble.

12 Write a description of yourself for a firm

Write your own curriculum vitae. Arrange it in the same way as the example on page 73, and use the same nine headings.

13 Write a description of yourself for a pen friend

Now write a description of yourself for a pen friend who is coming to stay with you for a few days next month, and who has never met you.

Write at least half a page.

■ ADVICE

Describing people

1 Start by writing a list. Include:

WHAT YOU LOOK LIKE
- You have to recognise each other at the station and you have no recent picture of yourself.

WHAT YOU ARE LIKE
- quiet, lively?
- hot-tempered, easy-going? (Warn your friend *now*.)

YOUR BAD HABITS
- smoking?
- always being late?
- watching too much television?
- eating peanuts and garlic?
- drinking beer with blackcurrant juice?

SOCIAL LIFE
- cricket club?
- discos?
- member of the local Mole Hunt?

---

2 Then rewrite your list as part of a letter to your friend.
One paragraph on each of the four headings given above would make your description well planned.

HOW TO DESCRIBE THINGS

You need a new saucepan — but cannot go to buy it yourself. You ask your young brother to get it for you.

The trouble is that he knows hardly anything about saucepans — and he doesn't *want* to know about them.

You know exactly the kind you want, but not its brand name, price or where to buy one.

You write your brother a list of its vital features, putting the main ones first:

> bright RED (like your new socks)
> with a LID
> ONE shade of red (NOT two)
> black NON-STICK lining
> RED handle, and lid knob (NOT black)
> 12 inches (31 centimetres) in diameter
> 7 or 8 inches (18/20 centimetres) high
> with a POURING LIP (to pour out liquids)

14 Describe something in complete sentences

Imagine you now have the red saucepan described in the list just given.

Using the same information, write a description of the saucepan, in complete sentences. (For help with this turn to Section 6 on page 83.)

Aim at writing roughly half a page.

15 Describe something using a list

You are sending someone to town to buy you:

a new cassette tape
or some hair dye
or some pyjamas
or a hand saw

Write a short list which describes EXACTLY what you want.

■ ADVICE

Describing things

1 To describe something more unusual than a saucepan you usually have to explain FOUR main things:

> what it **is for**
> what it **looks like**
> what it **is made of**
> how it **does its job**

2 Unless you are asked for **technical** details of how something works, leave them out.
Just give a simple explanation of how it works — for example, by pressing, melting or steaming.

16 Describing something in complete sentences

Write a description of ONE of the following, **using complete sentences** (not a list). Make sure that you explain the four main things about it.

> a tin-opener
> a wheelchair
> a steam iron
> an electric paintstripper or sander
> a portable electric hairdryer

HOW TO DESCRIBE PLACES

To describe a building, or any other kind of place — perhaps a park or even a town, you usually need to explain:

> **what** it is
> **where** it is
> **how big** it is
> **its atmosphere**
> **the kind of people** there

17 Describe a place

Describe a college OR a school you know well, for an old friend who is coming to live near you. Write at least half a page.

■ ADVICE

Describing places

1 Begin by writing a <u>list</u> of things you know about it.

2 Explain obvious things first, and more difficult things last.

3 Include:
> **where** it is
> **how to get there** by bus/on foot
> **the age group(s)** attending it
> **how big** the building is
> **how many** staff and students it has
> **the main subjects** or courses it offers
> **how successful** its students are
> **what kind of people** go there

4 Number the points in your list in a sensible order.

5 Lastly, rewrite your list as a description, in <u>complete sentences</u> and paragraphs. (For help with this, turn to Section 6 on page 83.)

---

18 Describe a place, using complete sentences

Write a description of any village or town you have lived in. Make sure you include:

> **what** it is
> **where** it is
> **how big** it is
> **its atmosphere**
> **the kind of people** there

Write at least half a page, and use complete sentences. (For help with this, turn to Section 6 on page 83.)

■ ADVICE

1 Begin by writing a <u>list</u> of everything you have to say.

2 <u>Number</u> the points in your list in a sensible order.

3 Rewrite these points, in complete sentences, using the order you have just worked out.

4 Words: work

Part of the Workforce

Losing your job changes you. Well, it's obvious: your pride is hurt, you're worried about money, and people either pity you or say you're lazy.

Of course the day doesn't start at 6.30 a.m. any more, when it's cold and dark — but that's about the only good part.

When it happened to me, I applied for every job that came up, from <u>foreman</u> at the shoe factory to <u>part-time assistant</u> at Jake's Joke Shop. I even tried for one job selling <u>agricultural machinery</u>, and I got an <u>interview</u> too. But they knew that I'd be no good at selling and I knew it as well. I know about <u>production lines</u>, <u>bonuses</u> and <u>piece work rates</u>, not about <u>sales targets</u> and <u>travel expenses</u>.

Luther Davis was made <u>redundant</u> at the same time as me, and he kept on talking about going to the army <u>recruiting office</u>. He did it too — joined up and went straight down south to some <u>training camp</u> near Bristol.

I began to think of trying the air force, but then I bumped into Gina. She was a <u>receptionist</u> at my old firm. She knew I was still <u>unemployed</u> and she told me she'd heard the <u>Personnel Officer</u> say how hard it was to get a <u>canteen supervisor</u> for the factory's <u>night shift</u>.

Within an hour I had seen the Personnel Officer's <u>secretary</u>, got the <u>information sheet</u> and the <u>job application form</u> and filled it in.

> I've never regretted accepting that job. I'm on the salaried staff now and the pay and conditions are both good. But I shall never forget what it was like when I lost my place as part of the workforce.

19 Words and spellings

Check the meaning, and the spelling, of all the underlined words in the 'Part of the Workforce' passage.

20 Think about the character

Write a **list** of ALL the information the writer gave you about himself.

21 List and describe the jobs

Make a list of ALL the jobs the writer applied for or thought of applying for.

Then choose THREE of these jobs. Write about five lines describing each one. **Write in complete sentences.** (For help with this, turn to Section 6 on page 83.)

22 Describe your job

Write a short description of a job you do, have done, or would like to do. You should write at least half a page.

■ ADVICE

1 Start by listing all the things you ought to include.

2 Then number all your points in a sensible order.

3 Now write the information out again using complete sentences. (Section 6 on page 83 will give you help with this.)

5 Check your punctuation: exclamation marks and question marks

EXCLAMATION MARKS

When you are: furious, shocked, surprised or laughing hysterically you don't plan what you say. Instead your words almost explode:

> Get out of here — and never come back!
> That's MY money you've lost!
> I HEARD you call me a gormless ferret!
> He keeps white rabbits in the boot of his Rolls Royce!

Exclamation marks <u>at the end</u> show these ARE 'exploding words'.

■ ADVICE

1 Put the exclamation mark <u>at the end</u> of your sentence:

> There's a man trapped under my wardrobe!

OR use one <u>at the end of someone else's words</u> when you repeat them:

> 'There's a man trapped under my wardrobe!' she said.

2 NEVER use an exclamation mark when you are <u>just reporting what shocked</u> or angered somebody else.

> She **told us that** there **was** a man under her wardrobe.
> (NO exclamation mark needed.)

3 Do NOT use a comma or full stop right next to an exclamation mark. (If you look at it, you will see it contains its own full stop.)

> 'That's crazy!' she said.

4 Use exclamation marks ONLY to show shock, horror, hysterics or something *really* unexpected.

> WRITE: I like curried icecream!

> but NOT: I like fish and chips!

QUESTION MARKS

A question mark goes <u>at the end</u> of a group of words to show that <u>those particular words</u> would be said in a questioning sort of voice:

> 'Is that chilli sauce you are drinking?'

■ ADVICE

The advice on question marks is almost the same as on exclamation marks.

1 Question marks go <u>at the end</u> of your sentence:

> 'Are you really going to buy that anorak with the red satin parrots on the front?'

OR use one <u>at the end of someone else's words</u> when you repeat them:

> 'Don't you like parrots then?' he asked.

Even when the QUESTION is at the start of the sentence, the question MARK still goes at the end:

> 'Are you going to eat that cream cake, even though you're on a diet?'

2 NEVER use a question mark where you are <u>just rewording</u> a question (instead of actually asking one then and there):

> He **asked me if** I disliked parrots. (NO question mark needed.)

3 Do NOT use a comma or a full stop right next to a question mark. (Again you can see that it includes its own full stop.)

> 'Haven't you any pickled peppercorns?ₓ' she asked.

23 Put in the punctuation

Most of the punctuation is missing from the following passage.

Write it out again, putting in:

> three full stops
> five capital letters
> two exclamation marks
> two question marks

— and set it out as THREE OR FOUR paragraphs, not just one.

> The bolts were loose. I knew those pipes were not coupled up properly and you can't take risks with scaffolding I thought I'd just have a quiet word with george, who'd fixed it extra fast on bonus rates he could put it right extra fast too, before the foreman saw it I'd just begun to explain when he started yelling at me like a maniac. 'Women surveyors' he screamed. 'You useless pack of trouble-making cowards. What are you interfering for. Do you think i don't know my job. I've been fixing scaffolding for years — ' Just then there was a crash like a double decker bus falling off the roof of an office block. But it wasn't a double decker bus. It was George's piping, closely followed by six planks, about ten courses of bricks and dave's wheelbarrow. all that was *nearly* closely followed by Dave, but the upright post had held. We stared up and saw him, wrapped around it and looking like a seasick monkey as it swayed wildly to and fro in the shockwaves, six storeys up.

6 Get it right: how to change notes into sentences

Notes are the skeletons of sentences. The bare bones of the meaning are there, but nothing else.

> 'Gone to shops. Back soon.'

This is fine for a quick note to stop your wife wondering if you have left home — but in most kinds of writing, 'skeleton English' needs extra words to put flesh on its bones.

We have no trouble with this when we talk to each other. You would not normally see a neighbour at the bus stop and say:

> 'Nice day. Early for work. Bus late. Going to walk.'

If you did, your neighbour might wonder whether you had a sore throat, or had just had half a pint too much. Instead you would probably say:

> 'Isn't it a nice day? I'm early for work and the bus is late, so I'm going to walk.'

The second version has just changed note form into complete sentences, by saying:

who is early for work **who** is going to walk	*and*	**it is** a nice day **the** bus is late

Here are some more examples:

NOTES	COMPLETE SENTENCES	
New bike, badly scratched.	**That** new bike **is** badly scratched.	
Going Fox & Hounds?	**Are you** going **to the** Fox & Hounds?	
Green trousers — orange stripes.	**I love** *or* **I hate** *or* **I can't find my**	green trousers with orange stripes
Jenkins, blue corner.	Jenkins **is in the** blue corner.	

Conversation (except exclamations)
Descriptions
Explanations
Letters
Reports
Summaries
Stories

} All need <u>complete sentences</u> (not just bare bones)

■ ADVICE

Check that each sentence makes it obvious **WHO** did **WHAT** and **WHEN**.

WRITE: **We have** been to see 'Kung Fu on Ice'.

NOT: Been to see 'Kung Fu on Ice'.

WRITE: **She landed** a left hook on his jaw.

NOT: A left hook on his jaw.

Check that your sentence has not left out words like:
A, AN, and **THE**
when it is about just one person or thing.

WRITE: I heard **a** woman on **the** radio say that work was bad for you.

NOT: I heard woman on radio say that work was bad for you.

Check that your sentence has not left out words like:
I AM and **THERE IS** and **THEY HAVE**.

WRITE: **I am** fed up with fried cornflakes.

NOT: Fed up with fried cornflakes.

24 Change notes into sentences

Change the following notes into complete sentences by adding extra words.

If you need extra information, make it up.

> Been to Joe's
> Fifty pounds down
> Going home
> Another camel in the garden
> Thirty pence a tube
> In the corner pocket
> There's trouble at bus depot
> Ginger hair and a blond moustache
> Down to his mother's

25 Change sentences into notes

Change these sentences to notes. Leave in only the bare skeleton of the meaning each time.

I have just remembered it is Varetta's birthday and we haven't bought her a present. Please can you get her a pound box of Cream Tray before the shops shut?

I reach Heathrow tomorrow afternoon. I should like you to pick me up from there at three o'clock.

Please can you change all your money into American dollars?

Please get me three pints of milk and a small pot of cottage cheese when you go to the shops.

■ ADVICE

1 Imagine each one is an urgent message you have to write to a friend.

2 Imagine that all you have to write on, for each one, is the back of a matchbox.

FILL IN FORMS

FILL IN FORMS

1 Forms

HOW TO FILL IN A FORM

There can be few people who really enjoy filling in forms. It is a boring job and it can be quite difficult as well. Still, we all have to do it and, sometimes, filling in a form can lead to something good like a holiday, a job or some extra money.

When you have completed a form, you should be sure that:

- you have given all the information wanted
- the information is correct
- what you have written is readable

otherwise you might miss your holiday, lose a job or wait for that extra money.

If you are completing an application form for a job, you might want to make it look really smart but, usually, the form just needs to be clear and accurate.

1 Look at different forms

Collect a number of different forms. You can get them from the library, the post office and the DHSS. Some of them might have notes on how they should be filled in.

Look through the forms and talk about them with a friend. Use the following questions to get you started.

Are the forms easy to understand?
Are the instructions clear?
What information is asked for?

Why is it needed?
Do the forms have notes on how to fill them in?
If so, are the notes helpful?
Could you improve the forms?

■ ADVICE

1 It is easy to make mistakes on a form. You can write the wrong thing or run out of space in one section. Crossing out or squashing words in will look bad and could make the form hard to read. It is a good idea to fill in the form with pencil first. Then you can check the information and get the spacing right before you go over the words in ink.

2 Start with the easy bits of the form. Get your name, address and date of birth down. That will get you going and make you feel better. Remember that 'date of birth' is sometimes shortened to 'DOB'.

3 THIS SENTENCE IS WRITTEN IN BLOCK CAPITALS. You should normally use block capitals on a form. They should be easier to read than handwriting. Have a thought for the poor person going through hundreds of the forms. That might be harder work than filling one in.

2 Practise block capitals

Because we do not use them most of the time, it feels strange to write in block capitals — but it is easier to read. Have a go at using block capitals. Write your name and copy out a few lines from the paper. See if you can work out a style that is clear and looks good.

REFERENCES AND TESTIMONIALS

A form might ask you to give the name and address of **a referee**. A referee is somebody who knows you well enough to give an opinion on you. He or she might have to say if you are hardworking or honest. Check if the person is willing to be a referee before you put the name and address down. It can be very annoying to get an unexpected letter asking for a reference. An annoyed referee might write something bad about you or just not bother to reply.

Sometimes, you have to send **a testimonial** when you return a form.

A testimonial is like a reference but you will know what it says. Here is a short example of a testimonial:

> Irene Sanchez worked at Bestprice Supermarket, Basildon, from 1.7.89 to 10.10.91 as a Saturday relief assistant. At first, she did shelf-filling and cleaning but she soon moved to check-out duties. She was always punctual and smart. Her work was excellent and customers liked her friendly, helpful manner.
>
> Rajinder Singh
> Manager

Irene would have got this from the manager when she left the supermarket or asked him to write it for her when she knew she needed a testimonial.

3 Write a testimonial

Imagine you run a small newsagent shop. Carlton Forbes worked for you as a delivery boy for two years and helped a little in the shop. Write a short testimonial for him. He is applying for a job with the Post Office. You can make up any details you want.

If you are filling in a hire purchase agreement, you might have to give the name and address of a **guarantor**. A guarantor is somebody who knows you are reliable at paying back money you owe. It is vital that you ask before you do this because a guarantor might be liable if you get behind with the payments.

PERSONAL RECORDS

Most forms want information that you do not keep in your head. It is important to look after personal records — any information about you — and store them neatly in one place. If you can find them easily, filling in forms will be much easier and less likely to raise your blood pressure.

4 What do you know about you?

Here are some questions about you which might come up on a form. See if you can find out the answers.

What is your National Insurance number?
Which of the following diseases have you had?
measles
scarlet fever
hepatitis
chicken pox
mumps
What is the name and address of your doctor?
How tall are you?
What weight are you?
Where were you born?
What is the address of your nearest post office?
What is your postcode?
What is your telephone number with STD code?
Who is the head at the last school you attended?
What is the number of your bank or giro account?

Here is an example of a simple form correctly filled in. It is the sort of form you might fill in to draw out money from a savings account.

ORDINARY ACCOUNT	DATE	MONTH	YEAR	FOR OFFICE
Withdrawal	5	11	1989	USE ONLY

Account number 342 279   Amount £35.50
Amount (in words) THIRTY FIVE POUNDS FIFTY

Name (CAPITAL letters) MISS JANE BREWSTER
Address 12, IRELAND AVENUE, ALTON, LEEDS
Postcode LE14 6TY

Please sign in the presence of the paying officer who may ask for evidence of identity.
I acknowledge receipt of the above amount

Signature *Jane Brewster*

The form asks only for the information which is essential. Jane has to write her name in capitals so that it can be easily read. She also has to sign the form because a signature is more distinctive. She signs with the paying officer watching so there should be less chance of somebody else getting her money. The amount withdrawn is written in words and numbers as a check.

You can see there is a section on the form labelled 'for office use only'. This is quite common. Do not write in that section or you might have to fill in the form again.

You can see that Jane has written '11' in the month box rather than November. Of course, you can write the name of the month but there is not usually enough room for that in full so it is probably neater and clearer to use the number.

5 Fill in a form

Here is an example of a simple form, applying for a duplicate vehicle licence. Copy out the form and fill it in carefully. You can make up any details you need. You might think up something interesting for what happened to the old licence.

---

1 Registration Mark of vehicle for
  which duplicate licence is required

2 Name and address of Applicant

   ....

   ....

   ....

   ....

   Post Town ....

   Postcode ....

3 I apply for a duplicate vehicle licence for the vehicle whose
  registration mark is given above

Declaration
I declare that the current licence has been lost/destroyed/
mutilated/accidentally defaced* in the following circumstances
(give details) *Delete as appropriate

   ....

   ....

   ....

Date of expiry of current licence ....
Period of current licence ....
I undertake to return the current licence if it is found
Signature .... Date ....

WARNING: It is a criminal offence to obtain or attempt to obtain
a duplicate licence by means of a false declaration.

---

6 Invent a form

Make up a lost property form which could be used by a bus or rail company. It would be filled in by people who have lost things while travelling or waiting at a station or depot.

Remember to get all the important information, but do not ask for details that are not needed.

You can work in a small group or alone, but when it is finished let somebody else have a go at filling it in.

See if you can find a form which is actually used and compare it with yours.

Here is an example of another common type of form — the insurance claim. Philip had his radio stolen, so he is making a claim:

PROTECTIVE INSURANCE
Claim Form

Name PHILIP WATTS **Address** 145 RIVERSIDE HOUSE
CHESTERFIELD
SH12 6YH
Tel. No. CHESTERFIELD 45327

**Policy
Number** 34/SDR/43984

**Item
claimed for** Williams 234 RADIO

Age of Item 6 MONTHS

Value of Item £25

**Give briefly
the reasons
for the claim** THE RADIO WAS STOLEN FROM MY CAR AT ABOUT 3 PM
ON SUNDAY 23.6.90. I REPORTED THE THEFT TO CHES-
TERFIELD CENTRAL POLICE STATION THE SAME DAY
BUT THE RADIO HAS NOT BEEN RECOVERED. THE CAR
WAS LOCKED BUT THE THIEF FORCED OPEN THE
WINDOW.

Signed P. Watts **Date** 14.7.90

This is a very simple claim form. If you are claiming a large sum on your insurance, the form could well be more complicated and there would probably be instructions on how to fill it in, especially the section on reasons for the claim. Philip seems to have given sufficient details. If you were reading his form, is there anything else you would want to know?

7 Fill in a travel form

If you book a holiday from a travel brochure, you will need to complete a form. Get a brochure from a local travel agency and choose a holiday you fancy from those on offer. Then complete the form to book that holiday. Get somebody else to check the form to see if all the details are there.

Travel agencies employ staff who spend a lot of their time filling up forms for people who do not like doing it for themselves. If you get to like forms, that could be the job for you.

When you are filling in a form, do not worry if you cannot put anything in a particular section. If there is a space to write your telephone number and you have no telephone, put a dash. The dash shows you have not just missed out a part of the form.

APPLICATION FORMS

One of the most important and probably the hardest forms is a job application. Obviously, all the information has to be accurate but you will also want to make it impressive, especially if the job really appeals to you. Not all jobs need an application form. Sometimes a letter is enough but often you have to send a completed form and a letter.

You will want your application form to look smart so make your writing neat. You practised your capital letters in exercise 2 so they should be good. Some people type their application forms but that can be hard unless you are an experienced typist.

There is the question of what to write with. A huge range of pens is available in the shops so you have quite a choice. Felt tips are not recommended but fibre tips, roller balls and fountain pens can all look good. Cheap biros are not attractive and you can get a sudden blot. A good quality biro is acceptable.

There is a wide variety of colours too. You might prefer to try black or a dark green instead of the more common blue. You could also look at different thicknesses of writing.

Remember one thing. What impresses an advertising agency may not go down too well with an undertaker.

8 Make your form look good

Fill in some old forms with different types of pen. Try various colours and thicknesses and see which you prefer. Discuss your preference with somebody else.

Most of the information on a job application form is the same old stuff — name, address, telephone number, date of birth — but there are usually three sections which are not normally on other forms and these are very important. The sections are:

- Qualifications
- Employment experience
- Other information to support your application

You should try to write something in these sections. It does not matter if you put a dash in the box for a telephone number but you should at least try to give some information to support your application.

QUALIFICATIONS

Mostly, we think of qualifications as examination grades in GCSE, 'O' and 'A' levels or CSE. If you have any of those, they should certainly go down on the form. Most forms want you to give the examining board, the date you took the examination and the grade you got. This information will be on the certificate.

There are other qualifications as well. If you are applying for a job at a swimming pool, a life-saving certificate will be important to mention. You may have certificates from RSA, the City and Guilds, BTEC or Pitman's, or have gained a college certificate for completing a YTS or CPVE course.

In some cases, qualifications gained in a youth organisation like the Guides or Scouts will be useful to put down. If in doubt, put it in.

Every extra piece of information tells the person looking at the form something about you.

Remember to look after any certificates. You may have to send photocopies with your application and perhaps show the real ones if you get an interview.

EMPLOYMENT EXPERIENCE

Most people will have some of this. Even if you have not had a regular paid job, you have almost certainly had work experience at school or in a training scheme. You may have delivered papers or worked in a supermarket on Saturdays. Put everything down. It will give a better picture of you. Delivering papers means you can get up early in the morning. Even a Saturday job shows you know what a day's work is like. If you have had responsibility, say so. Perhaps you work in a bar and managed it for one week while the usual manager was on holiday. That piece of experience could make the difference.

9 What to include on the form

Make a list of all the types of work you have ever done. Include everything — full-time and part-time, paid or unpaid, permanent, temporary or casual. Try to remember all the details — dates, addresses, pay. Forms sometimes ask for those.

When you get on to the section where you give any other information to support your application, you should think very carefully. There must be something you can put. Ask yourself these questions:

What are my interests?
What are my hobbies?
What places have I been to?
What sports do I enjoy?
How do I fill my time?
What TV programmes do I enjoy most?

These questions should suggest some things which you could use. It is a good idea to talk over your form with a friend who might well think of some points you have missed.

EXAMPLE OF A COMPLETED JOB APPLICATION FORM

JONES & SPENCER PLC
Application for position as Sales Assistant

Name JANE MARY MACNAMARA   D.O.B. 20.3.72
Address 24, EDWARD TERRACE   Telephone MANCHESTER 342167
ERRENSHAW,
MANCHESTER,
MA12 8KL

Education (give dates)

APRIL 77 — JULY 83	ERRINGTON PRIMARY SCHOOL
SEPT 83 — JULY 88	ERRINGTON HIGH SCHOOL
SEPT 88 — NOW	SOUTH MANCHESTER TECHNICAL COLLEGE

Qualifications obtained (give dates)

JULY 88 NORTHERN BOARD   GCSE ENGLISH C
GCSE MATHS D
GCSE HISTORY B
GCSE BIOLOGY B
GCSE CHEMISTRY E
GCSE GEOGRAPHY F
AT THE MOMENT I AM STUDYING FOR A CPVE AT COLLEGE. I WILL BE FINISHED IN JULY.

Previous employment with dates and addresses of employers

JUNE 85 — SEPT 88	DAILY PAPER DELIVERY FOR	KHINDA'S NEWS AGENCY 33, WATER STREET ERRINGTON
JUNE 88 — NOW	SATURDAY SALES ASSISTANT	MEGASTORE TRAFFORD SQUARE MANCHESTER
MAY 88 — JUNE 88	WORK EXPERIENCE FOUR WEEKS	LODGE CHILDREN'S HOME LODGE LANE ERRINGTON
SEPT 88 — NOW	WORK EXPERIENCE	DONMAR SUPERSTORE CHORLTON ROAD MANCHESTER

Other information to support your application

I AM KEEN ON SPORT AND WAS A MEMBER OF THE SCHOOL NETBALL TEAM. I HAVE PLAYED A LITTLE AT COLLEGE. I ENJOY SWIMMING AND GOT MY BRONZE MEDALLION AT SCHOOL.

IN MY SPARE TIME I LIKE GOING TO DISCOS AND WATCHING TV. MY FAVOURITE PROGRAMMES ARE SOAP OPERAS, POP MUSIC SHOWS AND ANYTHING TO DO WITH ANIMALS. MY FATHER KEEPS PIGEONS AND I HELP HIM LOOK AFTER THEM.

FOR THREE YEARS, FROM 1984 TO 1987, I WAS A MEMBER OF THE
GIRLS VENTURE SCOUTS. I GOT MY FIRST-AID BADGE AND WENT
CAMPING TWICE, ONCE TO CORNWALL AND ONCE TO THE LAKE
DISTRICT. THIS SUMMER, I HOPE TO GO TO SPAIN WITH A FRIEND
FROM COLLEGE.

Please supply the names and addresses of two referees

THE MANAGER,	MRS R. HATTON,
DONMAR SUPERSTORE,	LECTURER IN CHARGE OF CPVE,
CHORLTON ROAD,	SOUTH MANCHESTER TECHNICAL COLLEGE,
MANCHESTER.	MANCHESTER.
MA19 6TH	MA12 7YG

Signed Jane McNanamara   Date 10.5.89

It is possible that Jane will have to write a letter of application as
well as fill in this form. She has given a lot of information already
though. Somebody reading the form will know about her education
and her experience of work.

She has also written something about her interests which will help
to give an idea of her as a person. If Jane gets an interview, she
might get some questions about her sport and the holiday she is
planning.

10 Fill in a job application form

Think of a job that you could do well and that you would enjoy
doing. Draw up an application form like Jane's for the job and fill
it in. Do not leave anything out that could help your chances.

CURRICULUM VITAE

A curriculum vitae or c.v. is an up-to-date description of the things
you have done that might interest an employer. You set it out under
a number of headings and add new things as they come along. It
is like a form that you make up yourself. (See also Unit 3, pages
72–74.)

2 How to find information you need

Everybody spends a lot of time asking questions:

What does it cost?	How many can I have?
Where is it?	Where can I find out?
What is available?	Who can give me the answer?

Those last two questions are very important. If you are looking for information, then you need to know where to go or who to ask.

11 Things to find out

Below are ten things to find out. Some you may know already but where would you go to find out the others? How many you can get?

Who is your local MP?
What are this week's top ten records?
Find five places for bed and breakfast in your area.
How much is it to send a 1 kg parcel airmail to Australia?
How long would it take to get to London (or Manchester)
     by train leaving midday on Monday?
Do you need a visa to go to Peru?
What film is showing at your nearest cinema this week?
What is the telephone dialling code for Dundee?
How old do you have to be to have a cheque book?
Where is the nearest place you could learn karate?

WHERE TO GET INFORMATION

You can get the information you might need from many different places. Below is a brief list of possible sources with an idea of what subject each might deal with.

- Citizens' Advice Bureau — your legal rights
- Local councils — housing, roads, parks and leisure
- Tourist Information Centre — hotels and tourist attractions
- Yellow Pages — businesses in the area
- Library — local history and events, general information
- Jobcentre — employment possibilities
- DHSS office — benefits available

12 Other places to get information

The list of sources given above is just a start. There are many other places and publications where you could find out things you want to know. See how long a list you can make.

BE PREPARED

Some information comes written down so you can take it away and have a close look at it. Sometimes, you get information by word of mouth, perhaps from a person in an office or over the phone. When you are talking to somebody like that, it is important to know exactly what questions you want answered. The person giving the information will not be impressed if you seem vague or confused, and you may miss out on some vital information.

Work out beforehand what questions you will ask

Barry is thinking of buying a motorbike from a local garage on hire purchase. He is going to the garage tomorrow. Tonight, he plans out the questions he is going to ask:

- What is the cash price of the motorbike?
- What deposit is needed?
- How long does he have to pay?
- How much are the instalments?
- What happens if he misses an instalment for some reason?
- What sort of guarantee is there?

13 Plan your questions

You see a cheap holiday in Spain advertised in a newspaper. The advertisement does not give many details so you decide to ring up the company to find out more. Prepare a list of the questions you would ask. If the answers are satisfactory, you will go to the travel agency and book the holiday, but you do not want to make the trip for nothing so make sure you get all the information you need.

HOW TO TAKE NOTES

When you get information by word of mouth, note it down. You may have a good memory but it is always possible to forget details. It is annoying to find you did not ask an important question but it is much more annoying to have asked the question and then forgotten the answer.

Here are the notes Barry took when he went to the garage about buying the motorbike:

> Cash price of bike £393
> Deposit needed £80
> Pay rest over two years £16.50 a month
> Bike guaranteed for one year parts and labour
> Insurance available against missing payments through
>   sickness or redundancy — cost £24.50

This information will help him compare this garage's offer with another. It would have been hard to remember all those figures without noting them down. Of course, he could have asked the garage to put the figures down for him. This is a good idea because they are more likely to stick to an offer put in writing. When you are getting information by phone though, you have to rely on your own notes.

14 Take notes

You need to work with somebody else on this exercise. Ask your partner the list of questions you prepared for exercise 13. He or she should invent suitable answers and you should take notes. Check your notes against the list of questions. Have you got all the information needed?

■ ADVICE

People who give information have to deal with a wide range of individuals. Some of these will be vague, some will be confused and some could be rude and bad-tempered. Try to be pleasant. You will do better that way.

15 Stay reasonable

Pretend that you are somebody at an information desk answering people's questions. Get somebody to approach you with an enquiry, acting in a rude, abusive fashion. You must stay polite however badly you are treated. How does it feel?

16 Getting information

Complete one of the following information-gathering tasks. You may work alone or in a small group.

a) Your friend Sasha is confined to a wheelchair and lives alone. Find out what benefits are available for her.

b) Somebody is going to spend a week's holiday in your area. Find out as much as you can about accommodation and entertainment during a week you choose.

c) Somebody wants to take a two week holiday in Bulgaria. Get as much information as you can which would be helpful in planning the holiday.

3 Ask the right questions

Sometimes you may be walking through a shopping centre and a complete stranger with a clip board will come up to you and start asking questions. You may be asked how you vote or if you like a particular brand of chocolate. The questions are supposed to be carefully designed so you will answer truthfully.

You have probably also seen questionnaires. You find them in magazines and papers. You answer all the questions to find out how fit you are or if you are good at parties. Here is an example:

HOW FOND OF ANIMALS ARE YOU?

Answer 'yes' or 'no' to the following ten questions:

1 Have you a pet?
2 Do you enjoy going to zoos?
3 Would you ban fox hunting?
4 Are you a vegetarian?
5 Have you ever given food to a stray animal?
6 Do you hate real fur coats?
7 Is your dream holiday a safari in Africa?
8 Do you know what the initials RSPCA stand for?
9 Do you think animals are better than human beings?
10 Are your favourite TV programmes the ones about animals?

If you answer 'yes' to all ten questions, then you are crazy about animals.
Over seven and you are definitely a fan.
If you answered 'no' every time, the cats and dogs should definitely steer clear.

---

17 Improve a questionnaire

Answer the questionnaire on 'How fond of animals are you?' Get other people to answer it as well.

Look at the results. Do you think they tell you much about people's views on animals?

Have a go at producing a different set of ten questions to test the same thing.

OPEN AND CLOSED QUESTIONS

All the questions in the 'Animals' questionnaire were **'closed' questions**. You could only answer 'yes' or 'no'. The questions in questionnaires are usually like that because it is easier to use the results. If you were asked 'How do you feel about animals?', there are many ways you might answer. It is an **'open question'**.

18 Open questions

Ask a few people to write 50 words in answer to an **'open question'**. You can use 'How do you feel about animals?' or make up one of your own. Read the replies. What do they tell you about the people's attitudes? If you used the 'animals' question, you could also give them the 'animals' questionnaire and compare the results.

19 Look at questionnaires

Find as many questionnaires as you can in magazines or papers. Complete them yourself and get some other people to do the same. Discuss what you think of them. Use the following questions to get you talking:

> Were the questions clear?
> Did you get bored?
> Did you answer the questions truthfully?
> Were the results predictable or were you surprised?
> How might you have improved the questionnaires?

CUSTOMER RESEARCH

Firms spend a lot of money finding out what people think about the things they make and sell. That way they hope they can improve and sell more. A company making a chocolate bar might ask people to rate it under a number of headings. They might have to give it a mark from 1 to 5 where 1 is the best and 5 the worst.

NIBBLES CHOCOLATE
Customer Opinion Form

Please rate the Nibbles chocolate bar on the 1 to 5 scale under each of the headings listed, by circling the number you choose. (1 is the best, 5 the worst)

Taste	1	2	3	4	5
Value for money	1	2	3	4	5
Availability	1	2	3	4	5
Packaging	1	2	3	4	5
Advertising	1	2	3	4	5

---

20 Customer research

Make up a customer survey like the one for the Nibbles bar. Choose one of the following topics or one of your own:

A local record shop
A TV programme
A cinema or football ground

Give the survey to a number of people and see what the results are. You might like to add an open question at the end of your survey to get other opinions.

21 Construct a questionnaire

Draw up a short questionnaire on one of the following topics. You could work alone but it might be better to be in a group so you can test your ideas. If you do not like the topics given, make up one of your own.

People's smoking habits
The kinds of TV programme people watch
How people use their spare time

When you have constructed your questionnaire, try it out on as many people as possible. Examine the results to see what you have found out and discuss your findings.

4 Words: money

Cash Flow Problems

I am very good at spending. Whenever I have a few pounds in my purse, I have no trouble getting rid of them. People tell me that I should save for a rainy day. I have tried but some tempting purchase always spoils things. Mind you, I do have a building society account. My grandmother opened it for me when I was two. I have not made a withdrawal for ten years. There is £8.73 in it. Last year's interest came to 49p. My dad tells me it is good to have a building society account. The society is more likely to give you a mortgage if you save with them.

This summer I want to have a holiday in Italy with my friend, Maria. We will stay with her relations there so we will not have any hotel bills. I still have to find the air fare though so I am paying for it on hire purchase. I have made the deposit of £18. The monthly instalments are £12.50. I am quite worried about what will happen if I cannot pay. Could I be declared bankrupt? I have never been in debt. I am always broke but never in debt. Maria borrowed the money for the fare from her bank. She is paying off the loan by a standing order from her account. The bank will sell her Italian currency when she needs it too. She has her salary paid into the bank every month.

She says that stops her spending so much and it costs her nothing as long as she stays in credit. Maybe I should get a bank account. I am not sure I could handle a cheque book though.

The Inland Revenue sent me a tax form to fill in yesterday. There are all sorts of funny questions on it. What is my taxable income? Do I have any insurance policies? Any investments? It is all very confusing. I think I will go out and buy a simple book of advice on financial matters. On second thoughts, I will not. I have no money.

22 Check the meaning

Working alone or with a partner, check the meanings of all the underlined words and phrases in the 'Cash Flow Problems' passage. Discuss what you think about the person who is talking and what advice you might give her on her money problems.

23 How to fill in an income tax form

Get some income tax forms from your local Tax Office. These forms come with leaflets on how to fill them in. Check through both forms and leaflets for words or phrases you do not understand. Use a dictionary or go to your nearest library to find the meanings.

Have a go at filling in one of the forms. You can make up details if you want. After you have finished, talk with somebody else about the form and how hard it was to complete. You might pass your comments to the Tax Office.

24 Questions on money

Write a list of all the questions which bother you about money. See how many you can get answered.

Just asking friends may be enough but you may have to get information leaflets from banks or building societies. Insurance companies and government offices might be useful places as well.

25 Make up a questionnaire on money matters

Using all the information gained in the last exercise, work out a questionnaire to test people's knowledge of money matters. Check on the results and discuss them.

5 Check your punctuation: commas and apostrophes

COMMAS

Commas break up sentences so they are easier to understand. They are like <u>short pauses</u> in speech. Here are four examples:

1 **Sledgehammer, Annie Thorpe's backing group, have just made their first single.**
2 **With a hundred pounds in the account, you get a higher rate of interest.**

3 The bank manager will see you now, Miss Marinaro.

4 I bought a pen, a pair of white socks, a jar of hair gel and an LP.

Read the sentences out loud and you will hear where the commas come. If you leave them out, the sense is harder to get. You must never put a comma at the end of a sentence. There you *must* have a full stop. (See also pages 31–32.)

26 Put in the commas

Put commas where they are needed in the following sentences:

a) I think Mr Robinson we can let you have the loan.

b) After paying the last instalment the motorbike a Kazuki 1000 was hers.

c) Please give me the leaflets on mortgages insurance savings and personal loans.

d) They bought two strikers one from Watford and one from Stoke on hire purchase.

e) Excuse me Kuldip may I see the insurance policy?

f) When you return your tax form you will get your coding Mr Reilly.

g) I went to the bank the building society the post office and two travel agencies.

h) The man an airline pilot changed all his money one thousand pounds into pesetas.

APOSTROPHES

Apostrophes are used for two jobs. They can show <u>possession</u>:

Maria's account = the account of Maria
the children's savings = the savings of the children
Mr Davies's interest = the interest of Mr Davies
the book's cover = the cover of the book

or they can show that some <u>letters have been left out</u>:

it wasn't = it was not
I'm = I am
they're = they are
he won't = he will not

People can get confused with it's and its .

They are two different words so there should be no problem:

| it's | = | it is | OR | it has |

The apostrophe shows that letters have been left out.

| it's | raining = | it is | raining | it's | stopped = | it has | stopped

Without an apostrophe:

| its | = | of it |

so you will see:

| its | place = the place | of it | | its | colour = the colour | of it |

27 Put in apostrophes

There are ten apostrophes in the following passage. Put them in the right places.

> Im going to the bank to buy some French francs. I wont be long. Its just round the corner. The francs very strong lately and you dont get many to the pound. Maria and I are going to Italy but well stop off in Paris on the way. People say its a beautiful city and its shops are some of the best in Europe. I just hope theyre not too expensive. Marias relations live in Naples. Her fathers cousin runs a café there.

Remember — just TEN apostrophes — no more, no less.

28 Punctuation and paragraphs

Divide this passage into two paragraphs. Put in all the full stops, capital letters, exclamation marks, commas and apostrophes needed.

> alans mad about animals his flat is full of them he lives in manchester and he works at belle vue zoo so youd think hed see enough of animals during the day hes a keeper in the bear house its hard work but alan loves it he wouldnt do any other job last week he had to cut the oldest bears claws it sounds dangerous but jobs like that are all in a days work for alan when he gets home alans work isnt over he has to look after his pets theyre two cats a dog a rabbit and a kangaroo the kangaroos a baby alans looking after it because its mother died he has to get up in the night to feed it theres no doubt about it alan loves animals its not surprising alans surname is lyon when jokers ring belle vue zoo and ask to speak to mr lion the operator puts the calls through to alan

6 Get it right: 'none' = 'not any'

The word none gets more work than it should. None means
not any, so if you write 'not', it should be followed by 'any' as in
these sentences:

    I did not see any in the garden.
    There were not any left in the cupboard.
    He did not give the dog any.

OR you can use none instead:

    I saw none in the garden.
    There were none left in the cupboard.
    He gave the dog none.

You also use 'any' after 'never' as in these sentences:

    I never had any luck with elephants.
    There was never any.

Nobody and nothing work like none:

    Nobody = not anybody
    nothing = not anything

So if 'not' is already there, 'anybody' and 'anything' should follow.

WRITE: I saw nothing
BUT: I did not see anything

WRITE: She likes nobody
BUT: She does not like anybody

29 'any' or 'none'

Complete these sentences by putting **any** OR **none** in the spaces:

a) He had _____ in his bag.
b) The bank manager never lent him _____.
c) I did not know _____ of them.
d) After the battle, there were _____ standing.
e) The magician did not have _____ in the freezer.
f) After the holiday, she had _____ left.
g) Chester never trusted _____ of them.
h) Maria did not want to go out with _____ of the brothers.

WRITE A LETTER

WRITE A LETTER

1 Follow a plan

Letters matter. A well-written letter might get you a job or, at least, persuade somebody to give you the help you need.

A letter should look good. Think about the paper you use and how you write.

Layout is important.

ADDRESS

A letter must have an address. It tells the reader where to send an answer.

The address should be written in full with the postcode. Here is an example:

Flat number	Flat B,
House name	'High Gables',
House number and street	15, Primrose Avenue,
District	Seaton Green,
Town	WORTHLEY,
County	Suffolk
Postcode	IP42 7BN

This has all the information. You will probably need fewer lines for your address but make sure it is full enough.

The address usually goes in the top right hand corner of the first page. Space it out well. It will look bad if it is squeezed up.

1 Set out your address

Write out your address as you would at the top of a letter. Is all the information there? Does it look good? When the answer to both question is 'Yes', use that layout on all your letters.

DATE

A letter should be dated. The date usually goes under the address. Here are some ways of writing the date:

15.10.88
15th October, 1988
15 October 1988
Wednesday, 15th October, 1988

The day of the week is not essential but you should put the year. Letters can be held up a long time.

At the bottom of the letter, on the left hand side, you can write the name and address you put on the envelope. This helps if the letter loses its envelope.

STARTING A LETTER

There are different ways of starting a letter. Below is a list of beginnings and when to use them.

Dear Sirs,	Use when you are writing to a firm but no particular person in the firm.
Dear Sir, **Dear Madam,**	Use when you are writing to a particular person in the firm, like the Personnel Supervisor.
Dear Mr _____, **Dear Mrs** _____, **Dear Miss** _____, **Dear Ms** _____,	Use when you are writing to a particular person in the firm whose name you know. 'Ms' can be used if you do not know whether a woman is married or not, or if she has asked to be called 'Ms'.

FINISHING A LETTER

There are two ways to end a letter. If you start 'Dear Sir', 'Dear Madam' or 'Dear Sirs', you end 'Yours faithfully'. With the other beginnings, you end 'Yours sincerely'. You sign your name last of all. Make sure it is readable.

THE ENVELOPE

The envelope will be thrown away but it is important. The name and address should be clear and the layout should look good. An example is given below:

> Mr J. Robinson,
> Accounts Department,
> Lancashire Chemicals,
> 46–52, Midland Road,
> PRESTON,
> Lancs.
> PR42 8TH

2 Address an envelope

Draw out the shape of an envelope and address it. Choose an address from the newspaper or phone book. Have a few goes and see which one looks best.

Here is a job advertisement:

> ### WALTON GARDEN CENTRE
>
> require
> a young person to do general work in the centre — 5 day week but some work at weekends. No special qualifications needed but an interest in gardening would be preferred. Apply in writing to:
>
> The Manager,
> Walton Garden Centre,
> HASTON
> WH12 4QT

APPLICATION LETTERS

An application letter for this job might look like this:

---

                               ① 125, Brooklands Drive,
                                      Cartmel,
                                      HASTON
Tel: Haston 4756 ③   WH14 8CP
                             ② 25 September 1989

Dear Sir, ④
    I should like to apply for the job advertised in today's
Haston Gazette. ⑤
    I am eighteen years old and I have just finished a Youth
Training Scheme. I studied horticulture at Haston Technical College. My work experience was at the Whitehouse
Market Garden in Clipstone. The owner, Mr Gordon, says
he will write a reference for me if you need one. ⑥
    I have always been interested in gardening. My mother
has an allotment and I help her there regularly. Our house
has a small garden and all the family work to keep it looking
good. ⑦
    In my last two years at Oulton School in Haston, I took
Rural Studies. It was my favourite subject. I would very
much like a job in a garden centre. ⑧ Working at the
weekends would not bother me and I would be prepared to
work hard and learn quickly. ⑨

                    Yours faithfully, ⑩

                    Peter Jones

                    Peter Jones ⑪

The Manager, ⑫
Walton Garden Centre,
HASTON
WH12 4QT

Things to note about this letter

1 Full address
2 Full date
3 Telephone number in case the manager wants to contact Peter quickly
4 The right start to the letter — Dear Sir,
5 Saying where the advertisement was seen
6 Information plus the name of a referee
7 More experience
8 Refers to school and shows keenness
9 Again shows willing
10 The right ending to match 'Dear Sir,'
11 A full signature
12 The address as written on the envelope

3 Write June Clark's application letter

Here is a job advertisement. Write June Clark's application letter using the information given about her. Use your own address for practice.

BARTHOLOMEW'S CIRCUS

need urgently somebody to help with the circus animals. These include lions, an elephant, horses and dogs. Applicants should be fond of animals and willing to work irregular hours. No particular qualifications are wanted but it will be necessary to travel away from home for long periods. Apply at once in writing to:

Mr Simon Bartholomew,
Bartholomew Ventures,
14, St Anne's Villas,
LONDON NW1 4WE

(This advertisement appeared in the *Evening Gazette* 14.10.90)

Information about June Clark

June Clark is 19. She is unemployed. She left school at 16, after taking GCSE examinations in English and Biology. She did a YTS course in catering and worked in a restaurant. Last summer she worked for six weeks in a cattery. She has a dog and loves all animals. She has kept hamsters, rabbits and cats in the past. She is cheerful and enjoys travelling about.

4 Write an application letter

Find a job advertisement in your local paper and write an application letter. You can either use real information about yourself or make it up.

REFERENCES

You may be asked for a reference when you apply for a job. You have to give the name and address of somebody who knows you and is willing to write a few words about you. The reference might say how well you work or that you are honest and reliable.

You should not give a person's name and address without getting permission first.

Here is an example of a letter asking permission:

---

                                              ① 43, Melrose Court,
Brampton,
DEANCHESTER

Tel: Deanchester 35441 ③   DE47 6YL

                           ② 14th August, 1991

Dear Mr Lincoln, ④
   I am applying for a job at the Rapid Printing Company. They have asked me to give the name and address of some-body who can give me a reference. They want to know if I am hard-working and reliable. May I give your name? I think you know me quite well as I spent six years delivering papers for you. ⑤
   The application has to be in by the end of this month so I would be grateful for an early answer. You can ring me at the above number if it is more convenient.

                  Yours sincerely, ⑥

                  Delroy Brown

                  Delroy Brown ⑦

⑧

Things to note about this letter

1 Full address
2 Full date
3 Telephone number in case Mr Lincoln wants to ring Delroy
4 The right start to the letter — writing to somebody who Delroy knows well
5 Gives information and asks the favour. Notice that Delroy reminds Mr Lincoln that he delivered papers for six years
6 The right ending to match 'Dear Mr Lincoln,'
7 A full signature
8 The envelope address is not included. It is not needed in writing to an individual like this

5 Write asking for a reference

June Clark, who was applying for the job in the circus, needs a reference. She decides to write to Mrs Dobson who owns the cattery where she worked.

Using your own address, write the sort of letter you think June should send.

6 Write asking for a reference

Choose a job advertisement in the local paper. Write a letter asking a person you know to give you a reference for the job. If possible, show your letter to the person for comment.

7 Write a reference

Write a reference for somebody you know who is applying for one of the following jobs:

a) working in a large furniture warehouse
b) an assistant in a clothes shop
c) a gardener in a local park
d) an assistant cook in a busy restaurant

Be fair in your reference. Try to think what is needed to do each job well and whether your friend would fit the bill.

LETTER OF APOLOGY

Here is another example of a letter. It explains why the writer missed a job interview.

---

① 327, Harcourt Road,
WALLINGBOROUGH,
Hants. PO3 4QH

② 27 January 1990

Dear Sir, ③
   I am sorry I missed the interview for the sales assistant job yesterday. I was going to catch the 3.45 train to Portsmouth but it was cancelled because of the snow. ④ I tried to ring you from the station but the only phone was out of order.
   Today, I have rung your office three times but the number was engaged so I thought it best to write and apologise. ⑤ I should be grateful if you would arrange another time for an interview because I am still keen to work for Robinsons.

Yours faithfully, ⑥

Dawn Foster

Dawn Foster

Mr J. Oliver, ⑦
Personnel Department,
J. & R. Robinson,
Bridge Street,
PORTSMOUTH

Things to note about this letter

1 Full address
2 Full date
3 The right start — writing to a particular person who is not known well
4 Clear short explanation for absence
5 Shows the writer is still keen to have an interview

6 The ending to match 'Dear Sir,'

7 The address as written on the envelope

The letter is short. It says what is needed but does not waste the reader's time. It is sad that Dawn missed the interview but if Mr Oliver likes her letter, she might still have a chance of getting a job.

8 Write a letter of apology

You are on a package holiday in Spain. The travel firm which booked the holiday has gone bust and you could be stranded in Spain for an extra week.

Write a letter to the manager of the factory where you work, explaining why you will not be back at work on time.

9 Write for information

Here is an advertisement selling bicycles:

BIKES .... BIKES .... BIKES

Hundreds of bikes for sale at the same bargain price
All famous makes and
only £79 each

For immediate free delivery, send your cash today
to   BARGAIN BIKES,
PO Box 132,
BRADFORD.

(Make cheques payable to Bargain Bikes.)

You need a bicycle and you think the price is reasonable. Write a letter to Bargain Bikes asking for more information. Think of the things you would like to know before sending your money.

2 Make the right impression

A letter makes the right impression if the person reading it likes what is written. You write in a different way to different people. Here are two letters describing the same road accident. One is written to a friend of the writer. The other is for an insurance company.

146, Hackney Grove,
KETBURY,
Essex
CL3 4MB

18.8.89

Dear Sally,

I was in a car accident yesterday. The bad news is that my car is a write-off. The good news is that nobody was seriously hurt and it was the other driver's fault.

It was lovely here yesterday so I decided to drive to the coast. It only takes an hour on the new road and I was looking forward to a swim in the sea.

Well, I was nearly there when I had to turn right. I indicated and pulled into the middle of the road when I was hit in the back by this idiot driving at about a hundred miles an hour. He knocked me right into the path of the oncoming traffic and I was nearly bumped a couple of times before I could drive the car off the road. Luckily the engine was still running.

The man in the car that hit me leapt out and started shouting that it was all my fault. I was too shaken to answer. At that point, another man came up. He said he had seen the whole accident and I was definitely not to blame. He said the man who hit me had been driving much too fast.

Then, suddenly, a police car appeared and a couple of policemen got out and started taking details about what had happened.

Of course, I never got to the seaside. My car had to be towed to a garage and the police brought me home. They said they will probably prosecute the man for dangerous driving.

What a day! I am covered in bruises but it could have been much worse. I might even get a better car out of the insurance money.

I will write again soon to give you other news when I feel calmer. In the meantime, look after yourself.

Best wishes,

Madhur

Madhur

146, Hackney Grove,
KETBURY,
Essex
CL3 4MB

Tel: Ketbury 6254   18.8.89

Dear Sirs,

My car, a Ford Cortina QRT 379Z is insured with you. The policy number is AB3265. Yesterday, I was in an accident and my car was badly damaged.

At ten o'clock, yesterday morning, I was driving east along the A273. It was a calm, clear day. I was going to turn right on to the B360 to Offord and when I was about 50 metres from the junction, I indicated right and moved into the middle of the road.

Before I could turn right, I was hit in the back by a red Vauxhall Astra B363 CRQ driven by a Mr John Wilkins of 374, Walton Avenue, Comberton. He is insured with the Lancaster Exchange, High Street, Comberton.

My car was pushed into the path of the oncoming traffic and was nearly hit twice before I managed to drive the car off the road.

The accident was witnessed by Mr Lesley Smyth of 15, The Grove, Clacton. A police car arrived soon after and PC James Turner of the Essex Constabulary based at Clacton took details. He said that the police might prosecute Mr Wilkins for dangerous driving. Both Mr Smyth and PC Turner said they were willing to be contacted by my insurance company if that would help.

My car was towed to the Swan Garage at Offord and it is still there.

I should be grateful if you would let me know quickly what to do. At this moment, I am on holiday for a week but I return to work next Monday. I rely on a car to get to and from work.

Yours faithfully,

Madhur Singh

Madhur Singh

The Essex Insurance Company,
53, Queen Street,
COLCHESTER
CO34 8TY

10 How are the letters different?

Read the two letters written above and make a list of the differences between them. You could work with another person.

11 Write a friend's reply

Imagine you are Madhur's good friend, Sally. Write a letter to Madhur that would be sent about a week after getting news of the accident.

12 Write in different ways about the same event

Here is a description of a burglary which might have taken place at your home:

You are away for the weekend and come back Sunday night to find the house has been burgled. The thief got in through a broken window at the back of the house. A video-recorder and £30 in cash have been stolen. Two chairs were knocked over and there were muddy marks on the dining room carpet. You called the police and they are making inquiries. There have been a number of similar break-ins recently in your area.

Write the following three letters describing the burglary. You can make up any extra information you need.

a) to your grandmother taking care not to worry her
b) to a good friend making it sound as exciting as possible
c) to your insurance company claiming for things you have lost

DIFFICULT LETTERS TO WRITE

Letters to friends are usually easy to write but they can be hard sometimes. Here is an example:

16, Joseph Street,
Dingwell,
LIVERPOOL
L163 5NR

16 September 1991

Dear Dermot,

How are you? I have not heard from you since the holiday postcard. Are you enjoying life in Birmingham now you have managed to get a job? Mind you, it must be terrible not seeing Everton play.

I am still working but there is no overtime at the moment. I have decided to buy a motorbike and there is a chap at work who is selling a Suzuki 250. He says I can have it at the beginning of October when he gets a car. It will be a real bargain — only £150. I am saving up but I am still short of the figure. I wonder if you could pay me back the £20 I lent you before you went to Birmingham. With that, I would have enough.

Why not come up and see us the weekend after next? Mum says she can put you up. We could go and see Everton and have a few pints at the Queen's Head. I might be able to get the bike that weekend and you could have a go on it.

Look forward to seeing you,

Patrick

Patrick

Patrick has written this letter because he wants his money back. He makes it clear that he needs the twenty pounds but he also asks Dermot how he is getting on and invites him to stay for a weekend. It is a friendly letter and Dermot should not be offended.

13 Rewrite this letter tactfully

Here is a letter from Moira to her friend Gordon. He has asked to borrow her computer while she is on holiday:

143, Highland Court,
Lethbridge,
DUNDEE,
DU32 5NH

27 July 1992

Dear Gordon,
    No, I will not let you borrow my computer while I am away on holiday. It cost a lot of money and I do not want it broken. You are the clumsiest person I have ever known and I have no doubt that it would be a total wreck when I got it back. Do not bother to ask again.

Moira

This letter makes it quite clear how Moira feels but it is not friendly.

Rewrite the letter so it will not hurt Gordon's feelings. You must still say 'No' to his request. He is extremely clumsy, as Moira says.

14 Write a tactful letter

A friend's Alsatian has just had puppies. He has written to you offering you one. He is very keen that you should accept his offer and he says he will bring it up to you next week. You do not want a dog. Write a letter to your friend refusing his offer without hurting his feelings.

3 How to answer a letter

It is annoying to write a letter asking a particular question and to get a letter back which does not answer that question. Make sure you answer letters properly. Here is a letter that needs answering:

13, South Villas,
MAIDSTONE,
Kent
CA45 3TY

Dear Mark,

I have not time to write a long letter but I did want to say how pleased I was to hear you have moved out into a flat. What is the place like?

You are probably having a hard time affording furniture. I have a table, two chairs and a cupboard you could have if you want. They are in good condition. Let me know quickly because they are in the way here.

I would like to buy you something for the new home. What would you like? I will go up to £20.

Please apologise to your mother for me. Life is very hectic for me at the moment. There is a lot of work on and I am in the middle of decorating.

Best wishes,

Uncle Derek

The parts of the letter underlined need to be answered when Mark writes back. When you reply to a letter, have it by you. You can mark the parts which need answering and tick them off as you write.

15 Write Mark's reply

Mark reads Uncle Derek's letter. Mark's flat is a bed-sitting room, kitchen and bathroom on the second floor of an old house. He could certainly use any furniture he can get but, at the moment, he cannot think of anything to buy for the £20 gift.

Of course, he remembers to tell his mother that Uncle Derek is very busy just now. She says she will write to Derek in a week asking him to come for a weekend when he is free. Mark feels that this will be a chance for his uncle to see his new flat.

Write Mark's reply to Uncle Derek's letter. You can use the information given above or make up your own if you prefer.

16 Write a reply letter

Reply to the following letter, making sure you answer all the questions in it.

> Starlight Magazine,
> 100, Farringdon Street,
> LONDON
> EC9 4WW
>
> 20 February 1993
>
> Dear Reader,
>   You will be delighted to hear that you have won a star prize in our Holiday of a Lifetime competition. Your prize is a fabulous £1,000 holiday.
>   In order to organise your Holiday of a Lifetime, we need some details from you. Where in Europe would you like to go? You can choose any country you fancy.
>   Clearly, we want the holiday to be at a convenient time for you so please supply two possible weeks between April and October when you would be free to go.
>   Finally we need the name and address of your companion who will be sharing the Holiday of a Lifetime, and could you let us know if you want us to book a double room or two singles.
>
>   Yours faithfully,
>   *Janice Wilson*
>   Starlight Magazine

Here is a short letter from a firm:

Denton Mail Order,
PO Box 142,
PRESTON,
Lancs. PR5 2BQ

Our ref: CK/FY/18   23 July 1991

Dear Mr Callaghan,

Your order BZ 35

   Thank you for your letter of 14 July. We have no record of receiving your order BZ 35 or the ten pound note you claim to have sent with the order. Would you please send us your copy of the order form so that we can investigate further.

      Yours sincerely,

      C. Knight

      Denton Mail Order

Mr S. Callaghan,
14, Mill Crescent,
TETBURY,
Glos. GL67 3WR

There are two points to notice.

First, this letter has a reference code — CK/FY/18. This is quite common in business letters and you should quote the reference when you reply.

Second, the letter also has a title — Your order BZ 35. Again, this is quite usual. It helps the reader to know at once what the letter is about. Mr Callaghan uses it in his reply:

14, Mill Crescent,
TETBURY,
Glos.
GL67 3WR

Your ref: CK/FY/18   26 July 1991

Dear Ms Knight,

My order BZ 35

Thank you for your letter of 23 July. I enclose a photo-copy of my order form as you asked. I do assure you that the order was sent on 12 May accompanied by the ten pound note as I told you in my earlier letter.

Yours sincerely,

Stephen Callaghan

Stephen Callaghan

Ms C. Knight,
Denton Mail Order,
PO Box 142,
PRESTON,
Lancs. PR5 2BQ

You will see that Mr Callaghan says in the letter that he is enclosing a copy of the order form. It is important to say this in case the two papers get separated. You can, of course, clip papers together in some way but you should still say in the letter what you are enclosing.

Notice that Mr Callaghan sends a photocopy of the order form. He keeps the original form because that is the only proof that he sent his order.

17 Write a reply to a business letter

Read the following letter:

Our ref: JB/CR/A   Banks Boutique,
                                           8, The Promenade,
                                           SCARBOROUGH
                                           SC43 6YT

                                           15 September 1989

Dear Ms Fraser,
    Thank you for your letter of 12 September. I am sorry you
had trouble with the dress you bought here while on holiday.
The buttons are usually sewn on more securely than that.
I enclose a cheque for £5 to compensate you for the diffi-
culty caused and return the receipt you sent with your letter.
    If you send me a sample of the buttons on the dress, I will
post you some spare buttons to replace those lost. Once
again, may I apologise for the inconvenience. We do our best
to get things right but mistakes do sometimes occur.

                    Yours sincerely,

                    Jeff Baker

                    Banks Boutique

Ms E. Fraser,
63, Burns Lane,
EDINBURGH
ED45 9WS

Ms Fraser is very pleased to get this letter and the cheque. She
writes back enclosing the sample button as asked. Write the letter
she sends to Mr Baker.

18 Write two letters — a reply and a complaint

You receive this letter:

Our ref: RC/23A

Make Music,
43, Market Square,
LEDBURY
HE41 7YU

13 January 1994

Dear _____,

Thank you for your letter of 6 January. We do have the album you mention in stock. It is available both on disc and cassette. The price is the same for either — £6.95 including postage and packing. Cash must accompany order.

Yours faithfully,

Anne Jackson

MAKE MUSIC

You decide to buy the album. Write your reply.

When you receive the album, you find it is the wrong one. Write a second letter to Ms Jackson at Make Music complaining about the mistake.

4 Words: family

A Get-together

My friend, Joe, invited me to his wedding. The ceremony was in a church. I think Joe would have preferred a registry office but his mother and father insisted. There was a reception after in the church hall. About eighty people were there. They were friends and relations of both the bride and groom — parents, grandparents, uncles and aunts, nieces and nephews, cousins of both sexes. The bride's father gave a speech about not losing a daughter but gaining a son. I got talking to Joe's Uncle George. He has just been through a divorce but he seemed in a good mood. Perhaps the six whiskies I saw him drink helped. At about six thirty, the bride and groom left for their honeymoon. The party broke up after midnight. Uncle George was staggering by then. Nobody in the family would help him so I walked him home to make sure he was safe.

19 Check meanings and spellings

Check all the underlined words in the above passage. Make sure you know what they mean and how to spell them.

20 Put in the right letters

Below are all the underlined words with letters missed out. Each dash is a letter. Complete the words:

Fr——nd, w———ing, ce————ny, re—————y o———ce, m———er,
f———er, re—————on, rel————ns, br———, gr——m, p———nts,
un———s, a—nts, n———es, ne————s, c——s—ns, d————ter, s—n,
div————, h—n——m——n, fam———.

21 Complete the sentences

Look at this family tree, then complete the sentences below.

Example: John is David's <u>father</u>

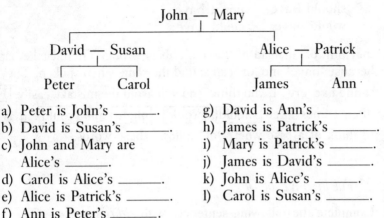

a) Peter is John's _____.
b) David is Susan's _____.
c) John and Mary are Alice's _____.
d) Carol is Alice's _____.
e) Alice is Patrick's _____.
f) Ann is Peter's _____.

g) David is Ann's _____.
h) James is Patrick's _____.
i) Mary is Patrick's _____.
j) James is David's _____.
k) John is Alice's _____.
l) Carol is Susan's _____.

5 How to set out a letter

22 Set out the letter

Here is a complete letter in a single paragraph. Write it out using the correct layout.

Put it in paragraphs and put full stops, capital letters, commas and apostrophes where needed.

Your ref: AB/27 122 king street trafford manchester Mc21 8nb 27 september 1993 dear sir <u>order no 63</u> thank you for your letter of 19 september returning the cheque I sent with this order I am sorry I forgot to sign the cheque I enclose a new cheque signed this time for twice the amount because I want to order two red sweaters rather than one would you please send your catalogue to my friend Ian Jenkins he lives at 142 morton road trafford manchester mc21 6tf and is interested in being an agent yours faithfully sarah grosvenor sales manager marlow mail order bridge street bradford br34 7vx.

6 Get it right: 'should have'

Sometimes, when people should write:

should **have**   might **have**
would **have**   could **have**

they put 'of' instead of '**have**'. This is wrong. The mistake happens because '**have**' and 'of' can sound the same when spoken. They both sound like 'erv'. If you think, you will avoid the mistake easily. [Have] often comes after [should], [would], [might] and [could]. It is hard to think of a case where 'of' follows these words.

23 Put in HAVE or OF

Complete the following sentences with *either* **have** *or* **of**:
a) The honeymoon would _____ been better in Scunthorpe.
b) The man in the pink suit is the father _____ the bride.
c) The groom's family and friends ate the food like a pack _____ hungry wolves.
d) Uncle Augustus is sitting to the left _____ Aunt Wilhelmina.
e) Her parents should _____ spent more than £2 on the reception.
f) My cousin Francis is the weightlifting champion _____ Essex.
g) We might _____ come to the ceremony but we did not get an invitation.
h) The divorce might not _____ happened but for his relations.
i) He could, _____ course, have married her mother instead.
j) The vicar could _____ made the ceremony shorter than five hours.

UNIT SIX

THE WAY
YOU TALK

THE WAY YOU TALK

1 Dialogue

Here are two people talking:

Kapil: Hi.
Susan: Oh, hello . . . how are you?
Kapil: Not too bad . . . could be worse.
Susan: You still at college?
Kapil: No, left there in July.
Susan: Working then?
Kapil: Got nothing yet but a mate of mine says they need people at the washing machine factory. I'm just off there now.
Susan: Mind if I come too. There might be something for me.
Kapil: Yes . . . come along. Be good to have someone to talk to.

This is a friendly chat between two people who know each other quite well. Most of the talking we do is like that.

1 Write a dialogue

Write a short dialogue between two friends. Try to make it real. Perhaps if you imagine two people you know talking, it will be easier. When it is finished, act it out with somebody and see how it sounds. You might tape it to get a better idea.

Most conversations are face to face. The people talking can see smiles and gestures which help the talk. **Telephone conversations** are more difficult even if the two people are good friends. If they are total strangers, the conversation can take a long time to get going.

2 Talk without seeing

Have a conversation with somebody, with neither of you able to see the other. You could talk with a screen between you or both of you could be blindfolded.

After you have talked for a few minutes, remove the screen or the blindfolds and discuss how it felt not seeing faces. Of course, this is the way blind people always talk but they listen more carefully than most of us do to the tone of voice.

TELEPHONE CONVERSATIONS

Here are two people talking on the phone:

(*The phone rings. Margaret answers it.*)

Margaret: Hello, 27435 . . . this is Margaret Scott speaking.

Steven: Good morning, Margaret. My name is Steven Birch. You don't know me. Bev Simpson gave me your number.

Margaret: Oh, I know Bev . . . what's she let me in for this time?

Steven: She said you might like to help at a jumble sale we're running at the youth club this Saturday.

Margaret: I might . . . what time is it?

Steven: Two o'clock.

Margaret: That's a good time . . . no problem . . . I'll definitely help. I'll be there at half one. Is that all right, Steven?

Steven: Great — thanks a lot, Margaret.

Margaret: Not at all — I enjoy jumble sales. See you Saturday.

Steven: Yes . . . and thanks again.

Margaret answers the phone and gives her number and name straightaway. The number is important. If the caller has the wrong number, taking a long time to find out could be expensive. After all, it might be a call from Jamaica. The name is important, especially if many different people could answer the phone. A name also sounds encouraging and it gives Steven the chance to use Margaret's name.

Steven explains how he got Margaret's number and asks the favour in a brief but pleasant way. Although Steven and Margaret cannot see each other, the tone of the conversation is friendly. It is easy to imagine both of them smiling.

3 Rewrite a dialogue

Look at the conversation between Margaret and Steven. Work out how the dialogue might have gone if Margaret had been unfriendly or if Steven had been confused.

Either write the dialogue down or work it out talking with somebody else. Again you might like to tape the dialogue to hear how it sounds.

Sometimes, you are in a strange place alone and the phone rings. It could be an empty office where you are waiting for the person whose office it is. Of course, you might decide to let it ring but if you answer it, what do you say? Here is an example dialogue:

> (*The phone rings. Wayne is alone in the office waiting for Miss Khan to return. Wayne answers the phone.*)
>
> Wayne: Hello, this is Miss Khan's extension.
>
> Caller: Could I speak to Miss Khan?
>
> Wayne: I'm afraid she's out of the office at the moment. I don't know how long she'll be. Could I help?
>
> Caller: Yes, could you pass a message to her?
>
> Wayne: Yes ... just let me get a paper and pencil. Right ... go ahead.
>
> Caller: I am her flat-mate. Tell her I've gone to Scotland because my Dad's ill. There's a cheque for the rent on the hall table and I'll ring her before she goes to work tomorrow. OK?
>
> Wayne: Yes, fine ... I'll pass on the message. Hope your Dad's all right.
>
> Caller: Thanks ... bye.
>
> Wayne: Bye.

It was a good thing that Wayne answered the phone and took the message. If he had not known Miss Khan's name, he could have given the extension number, which is usually printed in the middle of the phone.

You often have to take a message or make a note when you are taking a call so it is sensible to keep a pad and pencil by the phone.

4 What was Wayne's message?

Look at the conversation between Wayne and Miss Khan's flat-mate. Write down the message you think Wayne should have passed on to Miss Khan.

5 A phone conversation

Get somebody to write down information on one of the following:

a car for sale
a job vacancy
a day trip to France

That person will then give you this information in telephone conversation. Act this out sitting each side of a screen so you can hear but not see each other. Make notes during the conversation and see if you get down all the information.

Your caller is in a hurry so there is no time to speak slowly or repeat anything.

AN UNHELPFUL ASSISTANT

Here is a face-to-face conversation in which one of the people talking is not being very helpful:

Customer: Excuse me, do you work on this counter?
Assistant: Yes.
Customer: How much are these jumpers, please?
Assistant: It says on the label.
Customer: I couldn't find it . . . (searches) . . . oh, £12.99.
Assistant: That's right.
Customer: Could I try on a size 12?
Assistant: We don't have any fitting rooms.
Customer: If I bought a 12 and it turned out to be too small, could I change it?
Assistant: As long as you brought it back in the bag, clean and with the receipt.
Customer: I'll take it then . . . here's £15.
Assistant: Haven't you got the exact money? I'm a bit short of change in the till.

It is surprising that the customer ends up buying the jumper rather than going to another shop with more helpful assistants.

In the conversation, it is the customer who makes all the running. The assistant never offers help or advice. It is almost as if the customer had no right to be there.

6 Make the assistant helpful

Look at the dialogue between the customer and the assistant. Work out how it would have gone if the assistant had been pleasanter.

Do not make the assistant too humble — just somebody who is normally friendly and helpful. You could write the dialogue down or work it out in discussion with a friend.

7 A difficult customer

Work out another dialogue between a customer and a shop assistant but, this time, make the customer awkward and difficult and the assistant helpful and pleasant.

It would be a good idea to act this one out. See if the assistant can keep calm and patient even though the customer is so awful.

Occasionally, both people in a dialogue are bad-tempered and nasty. This does not usually happen in shops except in comedy shows. Here is a short unlikely example from a restaurant:

Customer: Waiter, come here at once.
Waiter: I'll come when I'm good and ready.
Customer: I don't want any of your cheek. Just come and take back this steak and get me a decent one.
Waiter: Are you trying to tell me there's something wrong with the steak?
Customer: I certainly am. It's as tough as elephant hide.
Waiter: Look here . . . that's best steak, that is. There's nothing wrong with it.
Customer: It may have been best steak before your cook got his hands on it. You could sole boots with it now.
Waiter: You watch it. The cook happens to be my brother.
Customer: Well, he's as good at cooking as you are at waiting, isn't he?

Of course, they could go on for a long time but perhaps it is best to stop them there.

8 A bad-tempered dialogue

Work out a bad-tempered dialogue and write it down. You can use one of the following situations or invent one of your own.

> Two cars have bumped into each other causing minor damage. The drivers get out and argue about whose fault it was.
> Two people grab a bargain at a crowded sale. Each claims to have got to it first.
> Two music fans argue angrily about which band is the best.

When you have finished writing your dialogue, act it out with somebody to see if it is convincing.

INTERVIEWS

Probably the toughest face-to-face dialogue is the interview, especially if you are the person being interviewed. It can be quite hard on the interviewer as well.

The most common sort of interview is for a job but there are other sorts. You might be interviewed on television, by a researcher, or by the police, and being questioned as a witness in court is very much like an interview too.

Interviews are quite frightening but there are simple rules to help you do your best.

9 Think about interviews

Try and remember any interview you have ever had. Put down all the details you can recall. Use these questions to help your memory:

> What was the interview for?
> Where was it held?
> How long did it last?
> Who was interviewing you?
> What questions were asked?
> What answers did you give?
> How did you feel after the interview?
> Why did you feel that way?
> What was the outcome of the interview?

It would be good to discuss memories of interviews with a friend. Perhaps you could interview each other about what you remember.

■ ADVICE

Listen carefully to the questions
If you do not, you may have to keep asking the interviewer to repeat questions, or you may answer a different question from the one asked.

Say if you did not understand the question
Do not try to answer a question you did not understand. Politely ask the interviewer to explain the question.

Think before you answer a question
Some people feel they have to answer immediately the question has been asked. That might be all right if the question was easy but you need to think about a hard question before answering. Give yourself a few seconds for thought.

Stop talking when you have answered the question
Do not waffle on if you have given your answer. Stop talking and wait. If there is silence, say, 'I hope that answers your question' or 'Does that answer your question?'

JOB INTERVIEWS

It would take too much space to print out a whole interview. Twenty minutes of talk cover a lot of pages when written down.

Here is the start of a job interview. David Singleton is being interviewed for a job in a warehouse. The interviewer is Mr Riley, the warehouse manager.

(*The scene is Mr Riley's office. Mr Riley is sitting at his desk. David comes in and sits down opposite Mr Riley.*)

Mr Riley: Hello ... my name's Riley. I'm the warehouse manager. You're Mr Singleton?

David: That's right. I've come for an interview for the warehouse job.

Mr Riley: Yes ... I've got your form here. You're on the Job Training Scheme at the moment ... is that right?

David: Yes, I've been at the FE college and I've had two spells of work experience.

Mr Riley: Good, let's talk about those. Where were you working?

David: The first place was Houseproud, the DIY super-
           market on the Viking estate.
Mr Riley: What were you doing there?
David: First I was just stocking shelves, then I did a couple
           of weeks on a till and finally I was working in the
           warehouse.
Mr Riley: What did you think of that?
David: I liked it. At the end of my time, I was responsible
           for a part of the warehouse. I moved stuff into the
           shop when I got a requisition, looked after deliveries
           and put in orders when stock was low.
Mr Riley: Was the stock control system on disc?
David: What exactly do you mean — 'on disc'?
Mr Riley: Was it a computerised system you were using?
David: Oh I see. Yes, it was computerised and I had to use
           the computer.
Mr Riley: That's good ... we've got a computerised stock
           system here and it's useful if new people have some
           experience.

That would be just a small part of the interview. It would take a few
minutes only but David has made an encouraging start. He has
answered all the questions sensibly without going on too long.

Notice how he gives enough in the answer to keep the conversation
moving. When asked if he is on a Job Training Scheme, he does
not just say 'Yes'; he adds a little more information which leads on
to the next question from Mr Riley.

David is also confident enough to ask what 'on disc' means. It does
not make him look silly but he would have been very silly to answer
without knowing.

10 Continue David's interview

Work out some more of David's interview with Mr Riley. You can
make up the details but here is extra information to help you:

    It is a furniture warehouse.
    Stacking is done with a fork-lift truck.
    The stock is very heavy.
    David would be directly responsible to Mr Riley.

Act out the interview with somebody else. Have a go at both characters. Record your efforts and play them through if you want.

11 A job interview

Imagine you have applied for one of the following jobs:

> Care assistant in a retirement home
> Cook in a hospital kitchen
> Bar person in a hotel
> Gardener in a local park

Get someone to give you an interview for the job. It would be good if you could take the interviewer's role as well so try to interview another person for the same job. That way, you will get an idea of both sides.

Talk about the different experiences afterwards. You could record the interviews if you wanted but people may not talk naturally if they know what they are saying is being recorded.

INTERVIEWING A WITNESS

If you see an accident or a crime being committed, you might find yourself being interviewed by somebody from the police. In this case, you are trying to give as much information as possible. Obviously, you need to give accurate information only, although that can be hard.

12 Do you remember what you see?

Go for a short walk round town with a friend. When you get back, each of you should prepare some questions to ask the other about what you saw on the walk.

Ask each other the questions and compare answers. Of course, answers that match are not necessarily right but if they do not match, one must be wrong.

An interview is often used to find out what somebody knows about something. This is a common sort of interview on television or radio. You can find out about cooking from an expert or what it was like when the Titanic went down from a survivor.

The purpose of the interview is to get information, so the interviewer should not talk too much. It is the other person we want to hear.

The job of the interviewer is to ask questions that bring out all the information.

13 Get all the information

Interview somebody. You can choose any topic but here are some suggestions if you are stuck:

> The person's last holiday
> The person's favourite sport or hobby
> A TV programme which the person has seen but you have not
> Where the person lives

Remember not to talk too much. Ask questions to get the other person talking. You might like to record the interview to check how you did.

Change places and get the other person to interview you.

PERSUASION

Sometimes when you are talking you are trying to persuade a person to do something. A sales person might try and persuade you to buy double glazing or a politician might want your vote. The best sort of persuasion is based on reasonable argument but some people bully.

14 Persuade someone

Try to persuade a person to do something. Be reasonable and answer objections sensibly. Do not bully. Here are some possible subjects:

> to take more exercise
> to buy an encyclopaedia
> to emigrate to Australia
> to learn first aid

2 How to handle the situation

When you are talking with other people, you will be more confident if you look your best. Not everybody can look like Madonna or Tom Cruise but if you are going for an interview, you want to feel right.

Your clothes should suit the occasion. That does not mean changing your style. Wear something you like that will be acceptable.

15 What is your style?

Talk with somebody about your taste in clothes. Use the following questions to get you started:

> What are your favourite colours?
> Where do you go to buy clothes?
> Do you prefer casual or formal clothes?
> How did you choose what you are wearing at the moment?
> What would you wear to an interview?
> What famous person dresses very well in your opinion?

16 Designing

Have a go at designing an item of clothing. It could be a jacket or a skirt, or perhaps a hat or a pair of shoes. Show your design to friends and see what they think. When could you wear it and where?

17 Are they dressed right?

Get as many full-length pictures of people as you can out of magazines and papers. Imagine that these people are going for interview for one of the following jobs:

> Cook
> Fashion shop assistant
> Bank worker
> Garage hand

Do you think they are wearing suitable clothes? What changes would you advise? You can talk about hair style and make-up as well.

BODY LANGUAGE

What you look like and what you say are both important when you want to make a good impression. Important as well is 'body language'. Body language is all the movements you make when you're talking with other people.

Sometimes your body can send different messages from what you are saying. If you tell a friend that you feel happy but you have a miserable expression on your face, you might not be believed.

18 Body contradicting speech

Work out body language which would **contradict** the following statements:

> I'm going straightaway.
> I'm not a bit worried.
> You're my best friend in the world.
> It doesn't hurt at all.

What body language would say **the same** as each statement?

EYE CONTACT

When you are talking with people, you sometimes look directly into their eyes. This is called 'eye contact' and if used sensibly it can help the impression you make.

In this country, most people like occasional eye contact when having a conversation. People get concerned if you never make eye contact or if you stare all the time.

19 Eye contact

Have two conversations with a friend about something you have both seen on television.

In the first, avoid any eye contact. In the second, stare at the person all the time.

Discuss afterwards how each of you felt.

ADAPTING WHAT YOU SAY

You talk differently with different people. What you say to an eighty year old will not usually be the same as what you say to an eight year old. How you greet your boss will probably differ from how you welcome your best friend.

It is important to choose the right language for the situation. If you call the police constable who is checking your car 'nosey' it could go against you, and your mother might get angry if you kept referring to her as 'Madam'.

20 Adapt what you say

You are the driver of a car that has just been involved in a road accident. Invent the details of the accident and then explain what happened as you would speak to:

> a man from your insurance company
> a good friend
> the eight year old son of the people next door
> your parents
> a police constable who arrived at the scene of the accident

IMPROVING THE WAY YOU TALK

Your voice should be clear and pleasant. Don't worry about accents. It doesn't matter that you sound Jamaican, Cornish or Irish. An accent can make your voice more interesting and attractive. It does matter though if people who speak English cannot understand you.

Think about your pronunciation. Make sure that important letters in words are heard. Do not speak like a robot. Just take care.

Many people speak too fast especially in a situation like an interview where they feel nervous. If you gabble, you may be difficult to understand and you will certainly be less impressive.

Sit straight but comfortably, breathe deeply and take your time. Remember, don't feel you have to answer all questions instantly. Think for a second or two before speaking.

21 Talking too fast

This is the sort of thing someone might say at an interview:

> My name is Francis Robinson. I live at 14 Walnut Close in Brigthorpe. I'm nineteen and I left Brigthorpe High School two years ago. Since then, I've been doing a Job Training Scheme. Some of the time I'm studying at Bramwell Technical College but I've had two periods of work experience, one last year at Danby Dyke Mill and another this year at Lester and Flood in Brigthorpe. That's where I am at the moment.

Read this aloud a few times at different speeds until you find the speed which sounds best to you. You could record yourself if this helps.

Sometimes when you have a cold, your voice sounds deeper. When you are nervous, you may find your voice going higher than usual.

Listen to your normal voice on a cassette recorder. Does it sound too high or too deep? If so, try changing it. Speak higher or lower. You cannot make great changes but you can certainly improve.

Practise, using the cassette recorder. You will be surprised with your progress.

22 Help each other

Get a friend to interview you about something. Here are some ideas:

> Your favourite music
> The clothes you like
> Food you enjoy

Ask your friend how you were in the interview.

> Did I smile?
> Was my voice pleasant to hear?
> Did I speak at the right speed?
> Did I look confident?
> Was my body language all right?
> Was my appearance suitable?

Add any other questions you like and use the answers to do better.

Have another interview a little later on and see if your friend is more impressed.

Make sure your friend is the sort who will not just be critical. You need praise and encouragement as well.

3 Get your ideas across

Sometimes you are the person with all the information and you have to pass that information over to other people. You might tell a stranger how to get somewhere or give instructions to somebody.

If you are giving information, here is some advice:

- do not speak too fast
- use simple language
- do not talk too much
- use questions to check
- repeat important points
- use plans or diagrams if they would help

23 Give directions

Have a look at the map on the opposite page.

Give instructions on how to make the following journeys:

> from the college to the railway station
> from the town hall to the museum
> from the police station to the hospital
> from the museum to the shopping precinct
> from the post office to the college
> from the cathedral to the railway station

24 Pass on information

Read the article on the opposite page. Make any notes you need and then tell someone all you know about the group, Zigzag. Try to use your own words as much as possible.

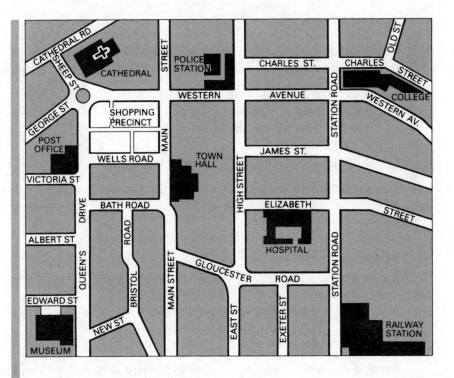

Zigzag are international in all senses. Each member of the band was born in a different country. The lead singer, Dan Lomas, is from the USA, Lena Marshall was born in Jamaica and Bill Van Prage is Dutch. Lena is the keyboards specialist and Bill plays guitar and saxophone.

Zigzag's latest hit — 'Cool Talk' — was recorded in Britain but the video which features arctic landscape was made in Greenland. Lena, the most talkative member of the band, says that they will be releasing an LP next year. She says that most of the songs are written and they have booked a recording studio for January in Sydney, Australia.

Meanwhile, the band are taking a holiday but they are not together. Dan is in Honolulu, Lena's gone home to Jamaica and Bill is skiing in Switzerland. The separation does not mean that there are problems. 'We all like holidays alone,' says Lena. 'We see enough of each other when we're recording.'

Anyway, there is good news for the band in their various haunts. 'Cool Talk' is Number One in the UK and in the USA. It's reached Number Three in Jamaica but, sorry Bill, 'Cool Talk' is nowhere in Holland.

25 Pass on information

Read one of the following, make any notes you need and then tell somebody what you have learnt. Use your own words where possible.

A holiday description in a travel brochure
An article in a magazine or paper
The information on the back of an LP sleeve
A DHSS leaflet
The details of a house from an estate agent

You might like to try another one for the practice.

GIVING A TALK

Giving a talk to a group of people is good experience. Start with:

- a group of about three or four people;
- a short talk of a few minutes only;
- a subject you know well.

Even if you know your subject well, prepare thoroughly. You can allow questions at the end so your audience can find out other things you know but have not told them.

You could also use a blackboard, pictures or objects to make the talk more interesting. People can get bored just listening all the time.

You should make notes for your talk but do not just read from a piece of paper. Check your notes when you need to but, most of the time, look at your audience and sound lively.

26 Give a talk

Prepare and give a talk on a subject of your own choice. The following suggestions might help you:

A game you play regularly
A town or country you know well
Any film you have seen recently

Do not make the talk too difficult for your audience. On the other hand, tell them some things they do not know already.

DISCUSSIONS

In a discussion, a number of people talk together about a topic.

In a good discussion, everybody taking part has a chance to say something. People listen to each other with interest and ask questions to find out what others think. Anyone who hogs the talk, interrupts or ignores other points of view will soon be unpopular.

27 Discussion

In a small group, discuss one of the following questions:

> What are the reasons for the increase in crime?
> What are the arguments for and against fox hunting?
> Are soap operas like real life?
> Are the sexes equal?

Some discussions are spoilt because people do not have enough information. It is difficult to talk about soap operas if you have never seen one or argue about crime if there are no facts available.

Of course, if you waited till you had all the information, you might never open your mouth at all. That would be silly but, certainly, it can be very useful in a discussion to have a few hard facts to quote.

28 Discuss, using information

In your small group, discuss one of the following questions.

Give yourselves time beforehand to find any information that could be useful.

> What food is best for you to eat?
> How could Britain do better at international sport?
> What makes people laugh?
> Is TV a good or bad influence on people?

Remember, you can get information from various places. You could go to a library, look in papers or magazines or just ask people.

Sometimes, a discussion is just fun. On other occasions, a **discussion can solve a problem**.
  If you were given some money, you might talk with a couple of friends to sort out what you should do with it. You would still make

up your own mind but the discussion would help you make the decision. Your friends would probably have ideas you had not thought of.

29 Solve a problem

Find a magazine you have not read and turn to the problem page. Choose a problem and discuss it in a small group.

> What advice would you give to the person?
> Is your advice different from that given in the magazine?

30 Solve a problem

Here are three problems. Choose one and discuss it in your group.

Work out what you think would be best to do. There are no 'right' answers but some make more sense.

> You are driving your car alone late at night along a lonely country lane when you collide with a motorcyclist riding without lights. The motorcyclist is knocked unconscious and seems to have broken a leg. Your car is damaged and will not go. What do you do?

> You are staying alone in a remote country cottage with no phone. On the TV news, it is reported that a dangerous criminal has escaped from a local high security prison. You go to bed but are awakened at one o'clock in the morning by a loud knocking at the door. What do you do?

> You are engaged to Lesley. One night you have a date but Lesley says she has to cancel it to look after a sick relative. You pop into a local pub to get a bottle of cider and there you see Lesley drinking with somebody else. They are obviously very friendly — kissing and embracing. What do you do?

GIVING A SPEECH

This is a hard job. Unless you are a politician, you probably will make very few speeches but there are occasions when speeches are expected and the following advice should help:

> **Make some notes on what you are going to say BUT do not read the speech — that will sound terrible.**

Keep the speech short.
Use your normal language and your normal voice BUT
do not speak too fast and
make sure you can be heard.
Avoid jokes unless they are very good jokes AND
you KNOW you are good at telling jokes.

You might be expected to give a speech at a wedding or when somebody is leaving a job. It might be you leaving and the other staff giving you a farewell party and present. One might give a short speech saying nice things about you and you will be expected to reply.

These might be your notes:

> Thank everybody for the present.
> Say how much I will miss working here.
> Tell story about the time I got locked in the store cupboard.
> Say good bye to all of them but mention specially the four
> people in my department — Dave, Ravi, Joe and Sylvia

31 Plan a speech

Plan a speech for one of the following occasions. You can make up any details you need:

> You have been given an award for saving someone from
> drowning.
> You are giving a present from the department to somebody who
> is getting married tomorrow.
> You are thanking a group of people who have raised a thousand
> pounds to send a close relative of yours for special treatment
> at a hospital in Switzerland.

4 Words: rights

Treat Me Right

I was talking to a friend of mine the other day. She told me she was writing to her Member of Parliament about the holes in her road. I said the local councillor was the person to contact. We got talking about our rights and she told me some things I did not know. Apparently, if you get arrested by the police, they can only hold you for a short time unless they charge you with an offence. You have the right to a lawyer as well. If you cannot afford one, there is the legal aid scheme which provides you with a solicitor free of charge. Of course, if you go to court, you might need a barrister but you can get one of them free as well.

I got quite interested in my rights so I went to the local Citizens' Advice Bureau to find out more. They were busy but one of the people there had a chat when things got a bit slack. He told me about my rights as a consumer. He said anything you buy has got to be in marketable condition otherwise you can get a refund. That applies to sales goods as well. You can cancel a hire purchase agreement within two days if you change your mind. He also told me about my entitlements to benefits through the Department of Health and Social Security (DHSS) and the National Health Service (NHS). I asked about income tax and he said that I had a tax inspector at the local Inland Revenue office and I could go and talk to the inspector about my tax coding.

I had a drink on my way home and got talking to a chap who had been given an eviction order by his landlord. The bailiffs were coming to seize his furniture. He did know what his rights were so I told him to go to the Citizens' Advice Bureau.

32 Check the meaning

Working on your own or with a partner, check the meanings of all the words and phrases underlined in the 'Treat Me Right' passage.

33 Are these rights?

Here is a list of 'rights'. Which ones do you think are truly your rights and which ones are not? Try and find out if your answers are correct. You could use a library or perhaps ask at a Citizens' Advice Bureau.

Everybody over eighteen has a vote.
Everybody in a full-time job must be paid more than eighty pounds a week by law.
Everybody has the right to free full-time education from five to eighteen.
Everybody has the right to housing.
Everybody over eighteen can stand for Parliament.

34 Who is in the right?

Read the following short stories. Which of the two people in each story do you think might win if the case went to law? Talk about your views with a friend.

a) A householder sees a man in the garden. There have been a lot of burglaries in the area recently so the householder assumes the man is the burglar and knocks him out, then rings the police.

b) A woman buys a spade in a sale. It is very cheap. After two days' use, the handle breaks off and she takes it back, asking for a refund. The shopkeeper refuses. He asks her what she expected for such a low price. He also claims she must have used it wrongly.

c) A car driver knocks down and kills a cat. The owner of the cat sees the accident and tells the driver he was driving carelessly and that there are two witnesses to prove this. The cat owner says he will sue the driver for damages over the loss of the cat.

5 How to set it out: inverted commas

Inverted commas are used to show that somebody is speaking. They go around the actual words that the person says. Here is a conversation between two people written down with inverted commas around the words they said.

Note that:
each new speaker gets a new paragraph

there is always a punctuation mark before the second pair of inverted commas. It can be a comma, a full stop, a question mark or an exclamation mark

"Hello," said Lerverne, "how are you?"

"I'm fine," answered Ravinder.

"What did the solicitor say?" asked Lerverne.

"She thinks I have a really good chance of getting my money," replied Ravinder.

"Good," said Lerverne, "you should get your money. It was definitely the firm's fault."

"That was what she said," continued Ravinder, "You ought to be a solicitor, Lerverne."

"That's not a bad idea."

once it is clear who is speaking, you do not have to write who said the words

35 Put in inverted commas

Here is a conversation between two people. Divide the passage into eight paragraphs and put in the punctuation.

You will need eleven pairs of inverted commas, seven full stops, three question marks and eight commas:

> Hello said Michael where are you going I'm going down to the Citizens' Advice Bureau replied Antonio Why are you going there asked Michael My mum's sick and she needs a home help said Antonio but the council say she's not entitled to one Can you do anything said Michael I don't know replied Antonio but the Citizens' Advice Bureau will know what her rights are I hope it's good news said Michael So do I

36 Put in the punctuation

Divide the following passage into paragraphs and put in all the full stops, capital letters, question marks, exclamation marks, commas, apostrophes and inverted commas needed:

> ranjit went down to the citizens advice bureau they were very busy but at last one of the counsellors was free what can i do for you she said i need some advice about this motorbike I bought answered ranjit well i should be able to help said the woman i used to work for a solicitor and i dealt with a lot of cases to do with consumer law whats the problem i bought the bike secondhand on hire purchase but it wont go said ranjit have you told the dealer asked the woman yes replied ranjit but he said i had no rights because it was secondhand rubbish snorted the woman you still have your rights as a consumer even a secondhand motorbike must go otherwise it wouldnt be in marketable condition will i have to take him to court asked ranjit i shouldnt think so said the woman just tell him youve been to see us he should be more reasonable thats a relief sighed ranjit

6 Get it right: 'did' and 'done'

When there is a ⎢have⎢ or a ⎢has⎢ around, you use ⎢done⎢.

When there is *no* 'have' or 'has' around, you use ⎢did⎢

So it is correct to write:

   I ⎢did⎢ it.

and it is correct to write:

   I ⎢have done⎢ it.

OR

   I've ⎢done⎢ it.

It is correct to write:

   He ⎢did⎢ the crossword.

And it is correct to write:

   He has ⎢done⎢ the job.   *OR*   He's⎢done⎢the job.

It is correct to write:

   The builders ⎢did⎢ the work.

And it is correct to write:

   The builders ⎢have done⎢ the work.

People sometimes write 'done' when it should be 'did'.

Every time you write ⎢done⎢ , check if there is a ⎢have⎢ or a ⎢has⎢ around. If there is *NOT*, you should have written ⎢did⎢.

37 Put in DID or DONE

Fill in the gaps in the following sentences with *either* **'did'** or **'done'**.

Use the advice above to help you make the right choice.

   She _____ what she could but he has not _____ the work.

   What _____ they say at the Citizens' Advice Bureau?

   The solicitor _____ her best.

   The baker has _____ nothing wrong so he cannot be charged.

   Anybody would have _____ what we _____.

   You can't have _____ it that quickly.

   I _____ what the DHSS told me.

   Both those cars have _____ more than twenty thousand miles.

   She _____ well then but she has _____ badly since.

WHERE TO FIND WHAT YOU WANT